Action

Professor Brown discusses one of the most difficult questions in metaphysics, "What is action?" His analysis proceeds along three lines: the point of view of the agent, the primacy of inanimate action, and the pervasiveness of explanatory insight in the description of action. As a whole, this excellent study gives an account of action in which the peculiarities of human action find their place in nature. A controversial theory of action, supported by careful argument, Professor Brown's work is both ambitious in scope and attentive to conceptual detail, and is a valuable contribution to one of the liveliest debates in contemporary philosophy.

D. G. BROWN was born in Vancouver and attended the University of British Columbia. He received his D.Phil, from Corpus Christi College, Oxford, was a Fellow at Magdalen College, Oxford, and since 1955 has been in the Philosophy Department at the University of British Columbia where he is now Professor of Philosophy. Professor Brown has had articles published in *Mind*, *Analysis*, *Philosophy*, *Philosophical Review* and *Queen's Quarterly*.

Action

D. G. BROWN

DEPARTMENT of PHILOSOPHY

The UNIVERSITY of BRITISH COLUMBIA

UNIVERSITY of TORONTO Press

© University of Toronto Press 1968
Reprinted in paperback 2014
ISBN 978-1-4426-5130-2 (paper)

This work has been published with the help of a grant from the Humanities Research Council of Canada using funds provided by the Canada Council. The author also gratefully acknowledges a grant from the Humanities Research Council in support of a leave of absence in 1958–9.

Contents

THREE / THE ORIGIN OF THE IDEA OF AGENCY

FOUR / THE ATTRIBUTION OF EFFECTS

I The point of view of the agent

1.1 *INTRODUCTION*

This essay offers a sketch of the concept of action. Some intuitive convictions of mine about the inner workings of the concept have determined the order in which I assemble the details of conceptual fact and examine the problems arising. In particular, there are three lines of thought which may serve to make intelligible the point of departure and the main divisions of the essay. These lines of thought concern 1) the point of view of the agent, 2) the primacy of inanimate action, and 3) the pervasiveness of explanatory insight in the description of action.

1) In ethics and in philosophy of mind, where we examine the justification and the explanation of human action, we can disentangle many problems by segregating for prior analysis such thinking as can be carried on from the point of view of the agent. By the point of view of the agent I mean roughly (see 1.9) that of the person for whom the question of what to do arises. It has become obvious through the revival of the study of practical reason that this is the point of view from which we must develop any logic of practical reasoning. I believe further that analysis of action carried out from this point of view can illuminate the relations of mind and body in

human action, and that the concept of this point of view enters into the analysis of the concept of human action.

I therefore devote Chapter 1 to an account of the point of view of the agent. Naturally the choice of this starting point, and the extent of its elaboration, must await judgment by their fruits.

2) My second line of thought is to take seriously the idea of inanimate action. It is presumably no accident that things done by stones or the wind are also called action, although there is very little theory in the field to account for the fact. But I incline to the more radical view that inanimate action is the primitive concept, and that in this as in other areas of the higher functioning of human beings we build on physical concepts the concepts of our various mental operations. Such an attitude might appear to conflict with my emphasis on the point of view of the agent as the distinctive feature of human action. But, on the contrary, it is just when we take up the point of view of the agent that the role of inanimate action forces itself on our attention.

Chapter 3 examines the way in which the agent himself finds a physical object, his body, to be the indispensable vehicle of his action. He is in fact a physical thing, interacting with other physical things, and the inanimate action of parts of his body is the basis of his interventions. The availability to him of the roles of inanimate things carries into his own action many of the structures of inanimate action.

An account which exploits inanimate action in the analysis of human action would lose much of its interest, and might be rendered incoherent, if it could be shown that some element of the concept of inanimate action had to be drawn from that of human action. For example, it is a commonly received view that the idea of natural causation is derived from anthropomorphic projection. Furthermore, even if it is proper to use inanimate action, the analysis of human action no doubt has essential elements of a distinctive sort. It might seem that if these ideas were accessible only to free and concious agents, they ought to reveal themselves in an analysis which is carried out from the point of view of the agent. Now it happens that both of these problems have been handled by an empiricist tradition which analyses ideas by seeking their origins. Chapter 4 treats both problems as problems about the origin of the idea of agency. The upshot of the investigation is that, by way of material for an analysis of action, we are left mainly with inanimate action, the role of the body, and the point of view of the agent itself. To make analytic use of the concept of the point of view of the agent, it proves convenient to abandon this point of view for that of the spectator.

3) My third line of thought could be regarded as an extension of a Humean approach to causation. I suggest that Hume saw inanimate action to be analysable in terms of the attributability of one event to another, and that this was a very Kantian insight into the way in which description of natural phenomena is pervaded by our understanding of why things happen. It occurs to me to extend this idea in the following sense, that from the point of view of the spectator we can regard human action as analysable in terms of the attributability to the soul of physical phenomena in the body or in the environment. For attributability to the soul entails the appropriateness of a whole realm of explanations, although these explanations proceed not in terms of causes but in terms of reasons for doing things. Chapter 4 attempts this Aristotelian extension of Hume, and uses the notion of attributability in a preliminary attempt to say what action is. It thereby brings the account full circle, since the organizing principle of the spectator's explanations of human action is the point of view of the agent.

Throughout the essay, while my theme is action, my guiding preoccupation is the faculty of reason. The investigation of the point of view of the agent is meant to help consolidate our recognition of an independent exercise of reason in action, and to contribute materials for study of the structure of reasons for action. My account of the relations between inanimate and human action turns at various points upon the analogies and disanalogies between practical and theoretical examples of thinking, of questions, of reasons, and of necessities. I believe that to reinstate the faculty of reason in our theory of human nature we need chiefly an adequate theory of modal concepts and of their relations to the various operations of the mind, from action to belief, which can have reasons for and against them. Finally, it is a major problem in our account of reason to exhibit the relations between causal explanation and those explanations of human action or belief which make reference to our rational nature. But in fact, to keep the essay manageable, I have made only scattered allusions to any of these topics in the theory of the faculty of reason.

1.2 A CATEGORY OF THINGS

Among the things which might be done, by anything, there are some things about which it makes sense to frame the question of whether to do them. Some questions that make sense are whether to go for a walk, whether to join a political party, whether to investigate a phenomenon, whether to let oneself yawn. Some questions that do not make sense are whether to grow older, whether to feel hot, whether to forget that one has a meeting, whether to wince. Let us consider the kind of thing about which the question of whether to do the thing does make sense.

The question of whether to do a thing can arise only for a possible doer of that thing. If it cannot make sense to the doer, it cannot make sense at all. The kind of thing just marked off must therefore be able to have a doer capable of understanding the question. If the range of doers extends beyond human beings, or even beyond human beings who use language, it does so only in marginal and problematical cases, like that of the ape wondering how to get the bananas. So for practical purposes we have a kind of thing which people can consider doing. It is a category of thing defined in terms of a kind of question.

1.3 THE QUESTION OF WHAT TO DO

There are many forms of question related to the question of whether to do some particular thing. These include the questions of whether to do this or that, what to do in a given situation, how to accomplish something, where, when, to whom, or with what to do something. The general phrase 'questions of what to do' covers the lot. For shortness I will sometimes use the term 'deliberation' more widely than in its ordinary use to mean thinking about questions of what to do.

To speak as some do of 'questions of the form "what shall I do?"' is suggestive of underlying grammatical structures, and useful for the analysis of some questions. But to insist on the forms of direct speech throughout the analysis of deliberation is to dramatize questions of what to do, and in payment either to lose generality or else to invent inner comedies and to overstress the asking and giving of advice.

If a question of what to do is to make sense, it must be possible to conceive of at least one person, and of at least one situation, such that in that situation the question arises for him. Whether or not, in that situation, he would actually consider the question, or even be aware that it arose, is not relevant. Thus it is clear that the question's arising is not a psychological event or state in the person. Unlike the statement that something occurred to him, the statement that a question arose for him does not imply awareness of any particular thing on his part. It is sensible to address to the person himself the assertion that a particular question of what to do arises for him, and to disagree with him about whether it does or not.

In formulating such a question no reference need be made to the doer, since that must always be somebody for whom the question arises. The question is somebody's question, and when one has specified whose question it is one has specified whose doing is in question.

There are two different ways in which a question of what to do can arise for more than one person at once. The question of whether to vote for the Democratic or the Republican candidate in the coming election for Governor of New York State arises for those members of that electorate who expect to vote. It arises for many in a common situation in that each is invited to consider how he personally is to vote. Similarly, the factual question of whether one can hear the actors arises for everyone in a theatre, in that each considers whether he can hear. In such cases, one can also say that there are many questions rather than one question, and that each of the many questions arises for one person alone. The question arising when I call for you at lunch-time of where to go for lunch arises for us together, rather than for each of us. We seek an agreed solution, and not merely coincident solutions which fortunately take us to the same place. Here there are not two questions, there is our single question, to which one process of joint deliberation supplies a single joint decision. Given that one is distinguishing among questions of what to do according to whose action is in question, one can say that the peculiarity of questions of what to do is that each one arises for a single individual or a single group.

If a man is considering what to do, he may invite someone to tell him what to do, or may put his question to himself, by asking 'What shall I do?' But there is no translation of this in direct speech, which substitutes 'he' for 'I', and if necessary 'will' for 'shall', so as to allow someone else to ask it. A man's question 'How tall will I be in a year?' becomes 'How tall will he be in a year?' 'Is it quite pins and needles that I feel?' becomes 'Is it quite pins and needles that he feels?' But if one asks 'What shall he do?', the question has changed, for one is asking someone in a position to give orders to give them, and not wondering what to do. And if one asks 'What will he do?', again the question has changed, for one is asking for a prediction, and not wondering what to do.

One can discuss a question of what to do, notice how it arose, or give advice about settling it, when it is someone else's question. But if one is actually to consider such a question itself, it must be one's own question, and must concern what one is to do oneself.

To consider in the abstract whether the question of whether to do something makes sense, is to consider whether the question is intelligible as one's own question. It is to consider whether one could in principle either contemplate doing the thing oneself or join in contemplation of the joint doing of it. It appears that we are dealing with a kind of doing mutually intelligible to its several agents; what one human being does, if the question of doing it arises for him, is in principle transparent to another, even though it may on occasion turn out to be as opaque as the other kinds of things which stones, insects, and people do.

1.4 THINKING AND CONFORMITY WITH REASON

Thinking can be thinking that something is the case, or thinking of a thing, or thinking about a question. It is this last kind which can be called inquiry, deliberation, pondering, wondering, and so on. For this kind of thinking, how exactly do we specify the subject-matter of our thinking? Evidently the subject-matter is specified by that which we are trying to do in the course of our thinking; namely, to settle the question or to find something that settles it for us. Our thinking about when an election is going to be held may come to completion when we learn the date set for it. Our thinking about whether to accept an invitation may come to completion when we accept. In the latter case, which is a question of what to do, the simplest outcome of thinking will be actual action.

But more needs to be said. Perhaps one would not deny the name of thinking to the most headlong flight from doubt and indecision, or to the most frivolous reaching down of an answer. It is nevertheless essential to any central case of thinking about a question that the person be seeking an outcome to his thinking which has something to be said for it, if only that there is nothing to be said against it. In other words, in thinking about a question, he wants a settling of the question which shall be in conformity with reason. Consequently, when he considers whether to do something, and goes on to ask whether such-and-such a consideration shows that he is under an obligation, or to reflect on whether he enjoys something, or to ask whether the situation demands a certain response, he has not left his original question but is still thinking about whether to do that thing.

The status of a *consideration* illustrates this general connexion between the notions of thinking and of reason. A consideration is something to be taken into account in one's thinking, and the recognition of it is, in the nature of thinking, a step forward. Yet at the same time, a consideration is something that tends to show that reason is on one side or other of the question. A fact will constitute a consideration bearing on a question just in so far as it constitutes a reason for making up one's mind about the question in one way rather than another. There is no such thing as relevant but neutral consideration; and the side it takes is, to that extent, the side that reason takes. Thus, for a fact to be relevant to a question is for it to have one of two things: either it has a tendency itself to settle the question in one way, or it has a tendency to give a man reason to settle the question in one way.

In that kind of thinking where the question is whether to do something, the process of thinking normally involves wanting to advance into possession of that which gives one reason to do or reason not to do the thing. One form of having reason to do the thing I have just noticed, namely that in which one has *a* reason for doing it. But it is important to notice that there are cases of having reason in which one has, and need have, no reasons.

It is not quite enough, then, if we are to say what deliberation is about, to say that the subject matter is defined by the question being thought about, and that the thinking seeks to settle the question or to find something which settles it. We have had to add that the thinking is directed towards an outcome which shall be in conformity with reason; it accordingly ranges over anything relevant, and is concerned to assess what bearing considerations may have on possible settling of the question. For the most straightforward cases, in which not even a time-interval intervenes at the close of deliberation, and the issue of it is actual action, we must add that the issue of satisfactory deliberation will be action in conformity with reason.

1.5 TWO FORMS OF QUESTION

It is worth distinguishing two types of question of what to do. They have in common a minimum requirement for an outcome of thinking about them, since for any question of what to do there are certain essentials for an outcome. They differ in the starting points they provide and the route which thinking must in consequence travel to reach its outcome.

The utter minimum for completion of any deliberation includes, first, at least one thing that might be done, and second, an outcome for or against it; the minimum for *satisfactory* completion includes some ground in the merits of that thing, i.e., includes reason for doing it or not doing it. Thinking directed to such an issue can now be divided according to the presence or absence in the question of reference to particular things that might be done.

For comparison, questions of fact divide conveniently into those to which 'Yes' or 'No' is an answer (e.g., 'Is it past three o'clock?'), and those which call for more (e.g., 'What time is it?'). The more is roughly material to complete a proposition, and, when provided, it allows one to form a yes-or-no question. Where questions of what to do are asked and answered in words, the same formulation holds. The answer may be 'Yes' or 'No', or it may be, to take simple cases, 'This' or 'That'.

But the distinction is independent of verbal forms for answering. On the one hand, there are questions of whether to do some particular thing. One's thinking is from the start concerned with a given thing that might be done, and leads towards a decision for or against doing it. One is normally concerned further with the point or purpose of doing it, and with any objections or justifications. On the other hand, there are questions of what to do, and in particular of how, where, or when to do something, in considering which one tries to think of particular things that might be done. These are typically questions of what to do in order to achieve an end. One's thinking starts from something to be achieved, or something desired, or some standard to be met, and has to turn up suggestions. It is in possession of that which would provide purpose or justification for the doing of something, and inquires into which particular action might take to itself, and bear, this purpose or justification.

We might state the task of deliberation in the two cases as: 1) given a possible course of action, to proceed via its merits to a decision for or against it; 2) given something at stake, to hit on a possible course of action that has merit in the light of what is at stake.

In one respect the first type of question is more fundamental. Any question about what to do in a particular situation, if it is to be settled at all, must be settled for or against some particular thing—except in the unusual event of a blanket decision to do nothing at all. If no particular course is accepted, nor is any even considered and rejected, the question of what to do remains unsettled. It follows that when, in considering the second type of question, one thinks of something to do, this suggestion may carry one, in the course of finally settling one's question, into considerations for and against the suggestion that are themselves not otherwise related to the original question. This reflection, that the outcome of deliberation involves the acceptance or rejection of particular courses of action on all their merits, casts light on an old difficulty about means and ends, and a consideration of that difficulty will cast light on questions of what to do.

1.6 DO WE DELIBERATE ABOUT ENDS?

One is inclined to say that we deliberate about means, but not about ends. This pregnant remark must be delivered of its offspring both sound and deformed.

There is a kind of deliberation which is at least typical, for which the dictum holds. Suppose, for example, one considers how to go about getting to know one's pupils, or what to read for an understanding of the situation in the Far East; or suppose the government considers how to stop tax evasion through expense accounts. Evening coffee parties may give the most time for talk; a suggested book may be a first-hand account but politically biased; abolition of expense accounts might provoke a *coup d'état*. Various means of achieving the ends in view suggest themselves; one weighs their merits, looks for alternatives, and decides between them. This is recognizably to deliberate about means, as it is wherever the question has one of a wide range of forms: how one can achieve something, what is the best way to do it, what one must do to do it, what one should do towards it, and so on.

This kind of deliberation not only is about means, it also precludes deliberation about the end. The question is in each case of such a form that it implies the intention, on the part of the agent whose question it is, of pursuing the end. This relation of implication is analogous to that between a question of fact and a presupposition of the question. There, the question does not arise unless something happens to be the case. Here, the question does not arise (say, of how to achieve an end) unless one has a certain intention (that of pursuing the end). The relations differ since that which is implied is within one's control, and one can make the question arise or cease to arise by forming or relinquishing the intention; to state that which one is implying would be to express one's intention rather than one's belief. But so long as one is in this way deliberating about means, one cannot be deliberating about the end, for then the implied intention would itself be in question.

At the same time it is clear that this kind of thinking about what to do involves thinking about whether or not to accept particular possibilities that suggest themselves. To do so will raise questions like: 'Is it worthwhile, or feasible, or legitimate, or within reason, to pursue the end in this way?' Such questions, and both positive and negative answers to them, still imply the intention. But an accumulation of negative answers may lead one to ask: 'Is there *any* means whereby it is worthwhile, etc., to pursue this end?' and finally 'Is this end worth pursuing at all?' At this point, the implication is no longer present, the intention had been undermined, and one is also deliberating about ends. That is to say, one is considering whether or not to pursue an end.

This possibility might be denied, and the dictum might be meant to deny it, on the basis of a theory about ends. It might be held that something becomes our end in so far as we want to achieve it, and that wanting something in this sense is an affection to which we are subject rather than an alternative presented to our deliberation. We cannot deliberate about ends, because it makes no sense to consider whether or not to want something.

But it is simply not true that if one wants to achieve something, then to achieve it is necessarily one's end. If one wants something, but is afraid to seek it in any way, one is declining through fear to make the getting of that thing one's end. If one lies in wait, hoping for an opportunity, one is not correctly described as having an end which one is not pursuing, but rather as being disposed to pursue or to adopt an end when the occasion arises. Even determination to achieve an end does not amount to pursuing it until some means of doing so has been adopted. In the case of ends, to be is to be pursued. A person's ends are, more fully, the ends of that person's action. Where there is no action which a supposed end is the end of, it is not actually his end at all.

It can, then, be a matter for deliberation whether to pursue an end, whether to adopt something as an end, and whether to abandon the pursuit of an end. According to the outcome of the deliberation, the things in question can come to be or cease to be one's ends.

This applies to ultimate as well as intermediate ends. One's reason for pursuing an end may be that one would enjoy the attainment of the end, as when a man works at his business because he enjoys having money, whether he can use it or not. To have money is one of his ultimate ends; he pursues money for its own sake. But he can still raise the question of whether to pursue this end, or to what extent; and on finding that its pursuit precludes that of other ends, or is morally objectionable, he can renounce this end.

This discussion has not yet exhausted either the dictum that we deliberate only about means or the attractiveness of the supporting theory about ends. There is a residue of at least the following points:

First, the intention to pursue an end is not normally either arbitrary or inexplicable. Typically (though not necessarily) one intends to pursue the end only because one wants to achieve it, and one wants to achieve it either because that would contribute to the pursuit of some other end, or else, in the case of ultimate ends, because one desires it, or would enjoy it, or thinks it would be pleasant, or something of that kind.

The connection can be looked at from the other direction. To desire something, for example, yet *not* intend to pursue it in so far as it was reasonably possible to do so, and in the absence of overriding considerations, would be irrational. Accordingly, if someone desires something attainable, the presumption is that he intends to pursue it, though the rebuttals of this presumption are familiar.

Further, when one is brought to ask whether an end is worth pursuing, so that the intention becomes subject to deliberation, one's new question still implies that one wants the thing one *might* pursue. Again, to abandon an end, on finding its pursuit not worthwhile, is to renounce something that one will in the nature of the case regret giving up. Again, one's reason for thinking the pursuit not worthwhile, e.g., that it is too expensive, or dangerous, or time-consuming, depends on the existence of other things one wants, which in the circumstances have become rivals of that thing whose pursuit is in question.

To sum up these points, it is normally one's wanting things that animates the process of deliberation both about means and about ends, both giving rise to ends and providing the point of any deliberation about ends. About these we do deliberate, but simply because the pursuit of one conflicts with that of another.

It remains to remind ourselves that often we deliberate neither about how to achieve an end nor about whether to pursue an end, but about whether to do some given thing. Nor do the considerations which are then relevant necessarily concern the achievement of an end.

1.7 THE STRUCTURE OF DELIBERATION

We have now established a bridgehead for the exploration of what it is that people must and may be thinking about when they think about what to do. This is, in a sense, to explore the structure of deliberation. But in just what sense? When a person actually deliberates, there is a stream of psychological events and states standing in various relations to one another. It would be legitimate to give the name of the structure of deliberation to the patterns of relations happening to obtain among these events and states under various conditions. Obviously that is not what I have been examining, nor have I needed any but abstract conceptual facts. But neither have I been surveying the range of logical possibilities for empirical structures of this kind.

The key to the relevant sense of 'the structure of deliberation' is this. What deliberation is about is defined not by what happens in the course of it but by the outcome which it seeks to reach. That outcome is, ultimately, action in accordance with reason. What I have been analysing, as for example in distinguishing two types of question, is no more than a set of complete or partial outcomes. One type of question holds out a possible justification, and calls for courses of action that might, by bearing this justification, constitute an issue to the deliberation. Another holds out a possible course of action and calls for a decision on it and for reasons that might complete the same end-product, action in accordance with reason. To say that a given person is at some moment thinking about one of these questions is to say what it is that would count as an outcome to his thinking, what part of this is already achieved, and what part is still to seek. It is to plot a direction and a point reached, and not to describe the means or the incidents by which the thinking moves.

To have reached the point of seeing that a certain fact constitutes a reason for doing a particular thing is itself to have reached a possible outcome. For in a case so simple that there was nothing more to be said, this point would be indistinguishable from doing the given thing, and for the given reason. But to have reached this point is also to have acquired one element towards the more complex results which are normal. Then one has reached a partial or an interim result in one's thinking. Moreover, progress towards a final result will depend on accumulating more such partial results.

It appears then that if we want to study, in one sense, the structure of deliberation, we can take as a basic unit of analysis the idea of a fact being a reason for or against doing something. For the structure, in this sense, is given by the outcome to be reached by thinking, and the basic unit in such an outcome is something to do or not to do together with a reason for or against doing it.

Where does one find facts which provide deliberation with relevant considerations? No doubt the facts of one's situation may be relevant. Indeed, there seems nowhere else to look. But why should only situation be relevant? It is natural to look for other factors, and natural to feel, on locating them, that one is still exploring the situation. This tension is due in part to the subtlety of the concept of the situation.

1.8 THE SITUATION

The question of what to do arises with respect to a situation, a situation which the person whose question it is either is in, or is to be in at the time of the possible action. We fall in very naturally with too crude a model of the situation and of its relation to the question of what to do.

The root idea of a situation, as of circumstances, is physical. Moreover, the situation in which one considers what to do often arises because of one's physical situation. We tend therefore to conceive of the situation as something which is to be opposed to the agent, and which stands in an obvious physical relation to him. But with reference to deliberation, the idea of the situation becomes more subtle, and so alters that the situation is rather to be opposed to the thing to be done, and stands in a non-physical relation to it.

Suppose a man finds himself at Bletchley station at 8:30 on a Sunday morning, with no useful train until the afternoon. This is a particular sort of situation one might be in. Here one is naturally struck by the surroundings in which one is physically placed. A visual picture offers itself; a man is confronted by his situation, almost as a house has a situation. A way to extricate himself from the situation is to pick up a ride on the highway and achieve physical distance from Bletchley. It seems that purely geographical description of the situation, though it might have to be complicated, could in principle be given.

But when considering whether or not to go out onto the highway, one regards the most diverse facts as facts of the situation. It is part of the situation that one is hungry, that one is not in a frame of mind to write anything, that one looks respectable enough to reassure a motorist, that there is no holiday traffic on the roads, that one has an appointment, that *if* one is late nobody will mind. There is not even a principle on which we could divide the facts of the situation into those that were and were not about oneself.

Even what a man is now doing is part of his situation. If one were standing outside the station dialling a number, that would be a fact of the situation. From the point of view of an agent, that which he is now doing is passing from his hands and adding progressively to the considerations which he can take into account in shaping his action. That I am now doing this or that may require that I next do so and so.

On what principle, then, can one select those facts that are properly called facts of the situation? Any fact counts as making up the situation which is or could become relevant to the question of what to do, and could be taken into account in considering what to do. There goes to make up a person's knowledge of the situation any fact known to him at that moment which he could take as a reason for or against doing something. The situation is therefore properly attached not to the person who is in it but to the thing he might do in it.

The cruder model of the situation sometimes bedevils interpretation of the principle that what is right for one person is right for
any other in the same situation. Surely what is permitted to some
men is not to others, and so on. But this principle speaks to the
condition of the agent, and from the point of view of a person
considering what to do, the sort of person he is (i.e., what the facts
are about him) is part of the situation. These facts will include what
he does or does not want. Kantian remarks, to the effect that duty
does not depend on what one wants, can and must be so interpreted
as to allow the fact that one wants something to be taken into
account like any other fact of the situation.

It would be too much to say that the situation consisted of the
facts that actually were relevant; there is no contradiction in saying
that certain facts of the situation do not bear on the question of
what to do. But it will usually be pointless to refer to the situation
at all unless the relevance of some aspect of it is in question.

1.9 THE POINTS OF VIEW OF AGENT AND SPECTATOR [1]

A philosophical usage has regained currency in which the points of
view of agent and spectator are contrasted. It serves brevity to
adopt it, but for clarity we must be more explicit about it. I offer a
partial analysis which I think to be that of the existing usage, and
then I will try in any case to make my own use conform to the
analysis.

In general, a point of view can be specified as being *of* various
kinds of thing, e.g., of a person, of a matter which is of concern, of
a subject or range of considerations. Thus: 'from the point of view
of the man's wife', 'from the point of view of his career', 'from
the point of view of morality'.

With respect to any question of what to do, the point of view of
the agent is that of the person whose action is in question, and
therefore also that of the person for whom the question arises. It
may happen that this will also be the point of view of a person who

1 With respect to the drawing of this distinction, and to the several
applications of it in later chapters (esp. in 2.7), I am grateful to Mr. Roy Edgley
for incisive criticisms which rescued the account from serious errors.

actually realizes that the question arises for him, or a person who actually considers it or comes to a decision about it. But the existence of this point of view is not attached to the actual occurrence of action or deliberation; it is attached to the intelligibility of the question of what to do, and to the satisfaction of the conditions for the question to arise in that situation.

That it should be the point of view of a person sets a limit on the questions that logically can arise from this point of view. What a person cannot distinguish cannot be distinguished from his point of view. Among other things, a person cannot at any time distinguish that which is the case, e.g., about his situation, from that which he thinks at the time to be the case. He cannot say to himself 'Certainly I am convinced that this is so, but is it so?', except by way of expressing his very losing of conviction. Later he will be able to distinguish what he *then* thought from what was actually so. At the time, he can foresee that he will draw this distinction; but this is only, at the time, to distinguish what is so from what he will later think to have been so. Consequently, if anyone else considers (say) whether the first person ought to do something, and considers it from the first person's point of view, he will not be raising certain questions which, looking at it from a different point of view, he could be raising. He will not distinguish between that which is the case and that which the first person thinks to be the case. To draw this distinction, when he cannot distinguish that which is the case from that which he himself thinks to be the case, would be to regard the other person as a different person from himself, and so to abandon the other's point of view. Where the other person is the agent it would be to abandon the point of view of the agent for that of a spectator.

The point of view of a spectator is that of a spectator *of the agent concerned*; that can be the point of view of anyone for whom the question does not arise, including the agent himself in a different situation from the particular one implied in his question of what to do. The contrast between these points of view coincides with that determined by the possibility or impossibility of distinguishing what then is the case from what the agent then takes to be the case.

At this juncture it might appear that the distinction between the points of view had in principle been drawn, but in fact the explanation of the distinction is still radically incomplete. For the explanation requires that in a consideration of a question by a spectator which the spectator carries out from the point of view of the agent, the spectator should suppress the distinction between what is the case and what the agent thinks to be the case. But this suppression can be carried out in favour of either limb of the distinction, by suppression of the other limb. It is therefore necessary to specify whether we are to disregard the facts or the agent's view of them; sound practical principles or the agent's practical principles; morality or the agent's morality. Certain purposes would be served by each of the two alternatives. The former alternative yields a distinction which is useful on practical occasions, while the latter yields a distinction of theoretical interest, which I will adopt.

Thus, suppose first that we disregard the facts, and in general the things on which the agent has beliefs, and keep to his beliefs. It is then natural to use an ordinary phrase like *From his point of view, the only thing to do was. . . .*' On this interpretation, when we consider matters from the point of view of the agent, we arrive at judgments prefaced by such things as 'Given his ignorance . . .', 'Granting that he sincerely adheres to that principle', and so on. (By such phrases we introduce various derivative senses of terms like 'ought'; I will discuss these senses in a moment.) Such judgments, and this interpretation of 'the point of view of the agent', are most serviceable in the practical business of arriving at a discriminating understanding of the actions of historical agents.

The second alternative is to disregard what the agent thinks, and to define the point of view of the agent as one from which we consider the actual facts and principles which are relevant to the agent's question of what to do. This is the alternative which I adopt. Accordingly, with respect to an action in the past, the point of view of the agent is that from which we reopen, so to speak, on his behalf the questions that the agent confronted. With respect to a request for advice from a deliberating agent, it is that point of view from which we urge upon him both our advice and the facts and principles on which we base it. With respect to the morality of any action, it is the point of view from which we arrive at our view of what, in the terms to be discussed shortly, is called the 'objectively' right thing to do. Such a definition of the point of view of

the agent thus selects an extended system of principles and of considerations generated by them, the theoretical interest of which is
perhaps obvious enough, but will in any case be further exhibited
in the next section (1.10). Roughly speaking, in such areas as tech-
nology, prudence, and morality, it is from the point of view of the
agent that we develop those systems of principles which furnish
the justification of proposed or actual actions and which lie at the
heart of those explanations of action which are the staple of our
mutual intelligibility (see 4.11).

The value of the distinction so defined will compensate for apparent paradoxes generated by a tendency for the ordinary use of the
expression to bear the alternative interpretation. Thus it will
happen that on many occasions on which one says 'From his point
of view, he should have . . .', one will precisely not be speaking
from the point of view of the agent in my sense. In fact I am left
with no characterization for the point of view referred to *within*
such a remark, even though the remark as a whole is, in any sense,
made from the point of view of a spectator.

Having explained the distinction, I now consider the range of
questions for which, by implication, the distinction has been
drawn. The point of view of a spectator, being defined by reference
to the agent, supposes, as much as the point of view of the agent,
the following: a question of what to do; relevance to this question
as the standard of what is relevant from this point of view; and a
situation or situations constituted by the facts which might be
relevant. Consequently, the contrast between the two points of
view is drawn only for certain cases of thinking or considering. The
question of how high a mountain is would not normally be considered either from the point of view of an agent or from that of a
spectator. On the other hand, if the question arises for someone of
whether to climb the mountain, the question of its height may become relevant; this amounts to saying that the answer to the factual
question can be taken into account (from either point of view) in
considering this question of what to do. In addition, given this
background, we can now distinguish between two ways of considering the factual question itself, namely from the point of view of
the person for whom the practical question arises and from the
point of view of a spectator. For we can distinguish the facts that

bear on the question of height from what the agent believed about those facts. But in the absence of such a background there is no distinction between points of view of agent and spectator with respect to the consideration of most questions.

Nor does the distinction apply to questions of what to do, since they arise only for the agent. We could say equally well that they had, tautologously, to be considered from the point of view of the agent.

What the field of the distinction does typically contain is questions of what must be done, can be done, cannot be done, or ought to be done. For example, one might say that since a mountain climber had in fact 2,000 feet to go, he ought to have turned back. Here one has considered the question of whether he ought to have turned back from the point of view of the agent, i.e., from the point of view of a person in the climber's actual situation. At the same time, one might be able to say that, bearing in mind the climber's firm belief that there was only 500 feet to go, he did what he ought (in another sense) to have done in continuing. Here, as a spectator, one distinguishes the facts and the agent's view of them.

The consideration of what someone ought to do from the point of view of the spectator gives rise to an array of senses for 'ought', as one chooses to take account of more or fewer of the possible distinctions between the agent's point of view and one's own. The sense of 'ought' generated in the example, with the analogous senses of 'right', 'obligation', 'duty', and the rest, would allow a resolution of Prichard's false issue between subjective and objective views of obligation.[2] For the judgment of what the agent ought in this sense to have done differs from a judgment of what he 'objectively' ought to have done only in taking as its basis the agent's view of the situation rather than the actual situation. Prichard asks which basis the obligation rests on; he ought not to have chosen an answer, but distinguished the senses and given each answer. But a discrepancy in judgments can arise either from misapprehension of fact, or from unsound principles of action, or from a misapplication of principles to facts, or no doubt in other ways. The only other sense of 'ought' which I am aware has been clearly

2 H. A. Prichard, 'Duty and Ignorance of Fact', in his *Moral Obligation* (Oxford : Clarendon Press, 1949), pp. 25, 28, 37.

identified in the literature is the all-in sense which takes account of all possible sources of discrepancy, and hence coincides with what the agent thinks he objectively ought to do. For this Richard Price offered the terms 'relative' or 'practical', as opposed to 'absolute' or 'abstract' (in place of 'objective'). He says that

> 'there is a sense in which it may be said, that what any being, in the sincerity of his heart, thinks he ought to do, he indeed ought to do, though contradictory to what, in the former sense, is his duty.'[3]

Elsewhere he says

> In one sense, *a man's being obliged to act in a particular manner depends on his knowing it; and in another sense, it does not. Was not the former true, we might be contracting guilt, when acting with the fullest approbation of our consciences. And was not the latter true, it would not be sense ever to speak of* shewing *another what his obligations* are, *or how it is* incumbent upon him to act.[4]

These two derived senses, Price's and the one I offer to Prichard, are probably the most important for ethics. They contrast in the following way. The question of what someone ought (relatively) to do is a straight empirical question, about what another person thinks, and one's answer to it, whatever the answer is, cannot be inconsistent with one' own principles. The question of what someone ought (in the other sense) to do requires one to apply one's own principles to the supposed facts, and in so far as these principles apply one will in consistency be committed by one's judgment to doing certain things if similar situations arise; it is a 'practical' and not an empirical question.

3 Richard Price, *A review of the Principal Questions in Morals*, ed. D. D. Raphael (Oxford : Clarendon Press, 1948), pp. 177–8.

4 *Ibid.*, p. 116 n. Cf. H. Sidgwick, *The Methods of Ethics*, 6th ed. (London : Macmillan, 1901), p. 207, where Sidgwick sees that the distinction cannot be drawn from the point of view of the agent. The harm done by Prichard is largely undone by K. E. M. Baier, 'Doing My Duty', *Philosophy* (1950). W. D. Ross sees the array of senses, in *The Foundations of Ethics* (Oxford : Clarendon Press, 1939), p. 162, but does not see that these distinctions are endemic among moral concepts and preclude any single answer to Prichard's question.

1.10 *LOGICAL SIMPLICITY AND IMPERATIVES*

Consideration of what to do, and in general the consideration of action from the point of view of an agent, has a kind of simplicity that is worth understanding. This simplicity can be defined by stating limitations on the ways in which one can speak of the doing of something and on the things one can say about it. It is instructive about the notion of doing something to see that the simpler type of discussion always applies to it, though the more complicated sometimes does not. In the course of explaining this double role of the concept of doing something I will try to show why it is attractive, even though it is wrong, to discuss action in general in terms of imperatives.

The question of what to do is not the question of what some particular person is to do (which might be anyone's question) but some particular person's question of: what to do. The doer does not need to be thought of, in considering the question, as partly defining which question of what to do is being considered; for the doer is necessarily the person considering the question. The question itself can thus be disencumbered of any explicit reference to a person. To say that I wonder what *I* shall do, or that he wonders what *he* is to do, is redundant, since both he and I wonder simply what to do.

Further, that which one can consider doing, when one considers what to do, is not capable of certain types of complexity. To give three sorts of example: 1) I cannot wonder whether to betray a secret unintentionally, or absent-mindedly, or accidentally. 2) I cannot wonder whether to buy something under a misapprehension as to its value, or whether to buy it by mistake, or whether to buy it for insufficient reasons. 3) I cannot wonder whether to publish something purely out of ambition, or wonder whether to publish it for the sake of duty.

These three kinds of complexity, all of which can be attributed to the things that people have done, are excluded in different ways from the things that one wonders whether to do. The first kind involves the failure of presuppositions of saying without qualification that someone did the thing; this kind of complexity cannot get into the question of what to do because it would at the same time involve the failure of presuppositions of considering the question. The second kind is founded on distinctions which, as I have explained, cannot be drawn from the point of view of an agent, and which therefore cannot get into a question which only the possible doer of a thing can consider. The third kind concerns the motives from which the thing will have been done when it is done; and since a determination of the motive from which something is done must take into account the considerations in the light of which the person did it, to include the motives in the question to be considered would generate a vicious regress.

I have been pointing out that some thinking about action lacks all complexity of these three kinds. But when thinking about action does possess complexity of these kinds, it is always possible at the same time to think about the doing of the same thing in the logically simpler way. For example, where a man has betrayed a secret accidentally, one can also ask whether there would be anything wrong with betraying a secret in such a situation as he was in. Where a man bought something under a misapprehension, one can also consider whether it was really worth buying. Where a man did publish something out of ambition, the question arises whether one would have published it oneself. In each case, the latter way of thinking about what was done is logically simpler, and none of the three sorts of complexity is represented in the way of referring to the thing done. That this application of the concept should be available always, and the other only sometimes, suggests that the simple conception of doing something is fundamental, and the complex conception, a superstructure.

The imperative mood of a word for the doing of something reflects the logical simplicity in question. The doer of the thing is not normally mentioned in an imperative utterance; for not merely are such utterances addressed to someone, but the person whose action is in question is by rule the person addressed. There is no need to mention that which is determined anyway by the conditions of utterance. Nor can one construct a sentence in the imperative which involves any of the three kinds of complexity discussed. At the same time, an imperative verb can stand as a complete sentence. An imperative sentence therefore can provide a complete utterance in which the doing of something is spoken of in a way that is logically bare.

This feature of imperatives seems to me the basis of the use made of them by Hare. No doubt they suggest themselves partly by their actual role in the giving of advice and instruction. But their actual role is so specialized that it should discourage one from any attempt to extend the notion of an imperative far enough to yield a complete account of the bearing of moral principles on action. Yet Hare is attempting at least that, for he tentatively proposes, in terms of an invented universal imperative mood, a complete analysis of moral principles.[5] This procedure provides him, first, with a guarantee that the concept of action shall appear throughout in a logically simple form, and second, with homogeneous complete utterances for a calculus in which the relations among principles, particular judgments, and action can be analysed in terms of a relation of derivability (his re-defined 'entailment').

Finding this extension of the imperative mood unintelligible, I have chosen alternative means of pursuing similar ends. Logical simplicity can be stipulated at any time (and the point of doing so is then made obvious) by adopting the point of view of an agent; and for the analysis of the relations among principles, judgments, and action, the ordinary concept of inconsistency has the needed range. As an example take the application, to a man's act, of the principle that one ought not to kill people, as expressed in 'He ought not to have killed her'. Hare would expound the force of the principle by saying that this application of it entailed a third-person past-tense imperative. This I fail to make sense of. But it is true to say that it *would have been* inconsistent to tell him to kill her while subscribing to the general principle. For just as it is inconsistent to hold (along with the principle) that it was right for him to kill her, so it would have been inconsistent to hold then that it was right to kill her. This in turn one understands by reference to the fact that it would have been (or was) inconsistent for the man himself, while holding the principle, either to hold that it was right to kill her or to kill her. If these points comprise what Hare is getting at, I can see why he might seek to organize them around

5 See R. M. Hare, *The Language of Morals* (Oxford : Clarendon Press, 1952), Chap. 12.

an 'imperative' imbedded in the principle. For these relations of inconsistency are traced from the point of view of the doer of the thing in question; the principle that one ought not to kill has practical bearing only because it mentions killing in such terms as one might oneself use when considering whether to kill. The general principle must contain the concept of something that one might do, and this concept must be simple in the respects described.

But, after all, imperatives have a sufficiently elusive logic of their own, before being asked to take on the work invented for them by Hare. By all means let us be aware that Reginald Jackson,[6] Hare, and the more formal writers on imperatives have rediscovered a continent, and let us join in exploring it. But it will save time, even where we need new concepts, to talk sense as we go along.

6 Let me cite, *honoris causa*: 'Practical Reason', *Philosophy* (1942); 'Rationalism and Intellectualism in the Ethics of Aristotle', *Mind* (1942); 'Kant's Distinction between Categorical and Hypothetical Imperatives', *Proceedings of the Aristotelian Society* (1942–3); 'The Moral Problem—the Problem for Conduct', *Mind* (1948).

2 The agent and his body

2.1 ACTION AND MENTAL DOING

The category of things which it makes sense to consider doing seems determinate enough.[1] But the definition of the category moves at a height of abstraction which leaves one short of breath. Somehow or other, having located this form, we need to understand where the content might come from to provide the instances for it. There are several ways in which we might try to do this. Can we say anything which holds generally for everything in the category? Can we find classifications broad enough to be instructive? Or can we locate nuclear cases, and trace instructive progressions from these cases to various groups of peripheral cases? A brief consideration of the first two possibilities will suggest that it is expedient to settle for the third.

First then, can we say at least, for the whole category of things which it makes sense to consider doing, that the doing of each of these things will fall within the category of action? The view has an initial attractiveness, and my definition of the point of view of the *agent* in terms of questions of what to do might be taken to carry this suggestion.

1 At this point I slide past difficult questions about the individuation of things which one can consider doing and the individuation of actions and the relation between the two. I am grateful to my colleague Ian Hacking for convincing me that my views on that subject were wrong, and to my colleague Howard Jackson for useful discussions, but the problem is too complex to be included here.

But in fact there are some exceptions, and an even greater number of hard cases. These occur when the doing of something is on particular occasions called 'mental', or when the thing done is naturally or necessarily done in a 'mental' way. Calculating the product of two numbers on a blackboard is certainly action, but calculating it in one's head seems to me not quite properly called an action. The calling up and dwelling upon a visual image has essentially some of the features which calculation can thus acquire accidentally, and it is clearly not action. Neither are the many kinds of thinking which can be called inquiry or deliberation or pondering, and which are typically but not necessarily carried on in a silent and withdrawn way. In fact it is here that we most easily draw a line of contrast between action and thought, and speak of thinking before we act, and of inaction due to absorption in thought. Calculating, calling up images, and thinking about questions, are all things which we can consider whether to do, and decide to do or not to do; yet the doing of them, sometimes essentially and sometimes accidentally, does not count as action.

Why not? Because the criteria by which the spectator tells what the agent is doing contain nothing about what is observably happening at the time. 'Outer criteria' there certainly are, but they concern, primarily, the circumstances and the ways of behaving of the agent over a considerable time, and secondarily, the agent's own report on what he does. There is a familiar difficulty with regard to mental events over explaining the kind of authoritativeness which attaches to the person's own account of them, and in reconciling this priority with his ultimate dependence, for his acquisition of the shared language, on the spectator's criteria. For the present, it is enough to identify this difficulty, and to characterize the cases in hand by saying that they give rise to it. When the doing of something becomes in this sense mental, it contrasts with the standard cases of action in just this respect, that it involves no overt behaviour. Bodily movement is no part of the doing, and indeed there is empirical evidence that the neural activity on which the doing depends can be entirely confined to the central nervous system. A standard case of action does, on the other hand, require the externally observable participation of the motor functions of the body. This is not to imply that most of the things we do consist mainly of bodily movement, as opposed (say) to the bringing about of physical or social effects. It is only to direct attention to the body as the indispensable channel of attributability to the agent of effects or consequences occurring beyond the body. The physical involvement of the body may dwindle to that of pressing a button or nodding the head, but it can disappear completely only when the doing of things is mental.

We have one of those situations in which we are strongly tempted by a general doctrine, and yet in possession of evident exceptions. There is the doctrine that the actual doing of anything we can consider doing is an action. Leaving aside any reference to the category of actions, there is the doctrine that every sort of thing we can consider doing involves the participation of the body. These doctrines seem hardly to lose interest through mere falsification by the examples of mental doing. Even the classification of the doing of things into mental and physical, and restriction of the doctrines to the latter, seems to correct the focus at the expense of losing some of the light. Commonly in such a situation, we have hit on a principle which holds for nuclear cases but not for peripheral ones. By dealing in classifications that separate the nuclear and the peripheral we can approach correctness. But in the long run the principle illuminates chiefly by identifying the nuclear as opposed to the peripheral, and by establishing priorities for the arrangement of our examples in an intelligible order.

I think it a reasonable suspicion, and one adequate to dictate the order of our account, that if we have a nuclear case of a thing which it makes sense to consider doing, then the actual doing of that thing will provide a nuclear case of action; and further, that if we have a nuclear case of action in the form of the actual doing of some thing, then that thing will provide us with a nuclear case of something which it makes sense to consider doing.

Some indication of the nature of the nuclear cases has emerged already. They seem likely to involve overt and clear-cut participation of one's body together with obvious physical effects of this activity. The area located is still large, and so much might indeed have been guessed on the basis of empirical facts about the relative ease of learning to do various kinds of things.

But a second line of thought leads to the same assignment of priorities. What else is called action, other than that doing which is or could be the outcome of deliberation on the part of the agent? Clearly the action of inanimate agents. As a matter of fact the parallelism between inanimate and human action, and especially the overlap between things which inanimate agents can do and nuclear cases of things which people can do, proves to be very extensive. But even verbally it is striking that there seem to be two main applications of the abstract noun 'action', one to a sort of thing for which people are held responsible, the other to a sort of thing which goes on in the simplest physical transactions in nature. The direct comparison of the two kinds of action invites attention in its own right. But further, we can use the notion of inanimate action to restate the preceding considerations: a nuclear case of human action involves the inanimate action of the agent's body.

This dictum stands, at least, if we admit that the agent's hand or foot is merely part of an animate thing and is itself an inanimate thing. If it stretches the words too much to call a hand either animate or inanimate, the point can be restarted as follows. A nuclear case of human action involves the action of some part of the agent's body on something in his surroundings, and this latter action, although its origin and explanation are special, does not in itself differ from the action of stones and water.

Of course it is plausible to regard either human action or inanimate action as fundamental to the other. A received view is that to speak at all of inanimate action, if not actually improper, is a metaphor founded on the notion of human action, and in either case is anthropomorphic. This view deserves exploration, and an understanding of its attractiveness and its perversity happens to yield insights about the role of modal concepts in the theory of reasons for action. I therefore leave it now, and give the first half of Chapter 3 to my attack on it.

In the meantime I take at face value the idea of inanimate action, and try the effect of selecting, as probably nuclear cases of things which a person can consider doing, things which he can observe being done in the action of inanimate agents. My enterprise is still to maintain the point of view of an agent, and from his point of view to survey the range of things which he can consider doing. It is precisely to this end that I draw upon the notion of inanimate action as an independently available concept for exploitation in the analysis.

Without foreseeing the course of the analysis, there is a presumption in favour of this order. To a disinterested observer of nature it might seem that among the incessant interactions of inanimate things, and at a particular period of time, there appeared agents the sources of whose action were especially complex, in the ways implied by attributing to anything what Aristotle called a soul; and that however extraordinary the range of animate action might prove to be, the peculiarities of such action were built upon the characteristics of inanimate action. In a matter of the bending of a branch, I am substitutable for the wind; and it is my body, and the inanimate action of its parts, that accounts for this role being open to me. My embodiment is my access to the field of natural action. This necessity of being embodied, if I am to get anything done, is the key to understanding the way in which the concept of inanimate action is primitive for the analysis of the concept of animate action.

2.2 INANIMATE ACTION AND THE PRODUCING OF EFFECTS

Inanimate action has the peculiarity that it is always *on* something. Among the various things which the wind, or stones, or water can do, those which can be called action consist of these agents doing something *to* something else. The action of the wind is what it does *to* the surface of the lake or *to* the leaves of a tree; the action of the stones of a beach might be *on* bits of glass which they grind to powder; the action of the sun *on* the stones might be to warm them. If a stone merely falls, or the sun merely rises, that is not action.

We seem not to speak in the plural of the action*s* of inanimate agents. Perhaps the reason is that we tend in fact to be largely concerned with natural action in the abstract or as pure instances of its types, and accordingly see any given instance of it as one more recurrence of the type rather than one more action of a concrete particular. We accordingly tend to identify as natural agents either substances, in the sense of kinds of stuff, such as sulphuric acid or aspirin; or phenomena, in the sense of kinds of things that recur, such as frost or radiation; or things of a comparable level. Last night's wreckage in the woods is due rather to last night's action of (the) wind than to the action of last night's wind. It would become natural to individuate the actions of last night's wind to the extent that we followed its particular identity through an extended history. The still somewhat faltering operation of the plural in its strongest application, to human action, is possible only through our highly organized concern with personal identity.

These linguistic points about 'action', together with corresponding ones about the verb 'act', turn out to be faithful guides in exploring a wide range of specific concepts. I now select a group of verbs which can clearly be terms for kinds of action of one thing on another, and which are differentiated by possession of two characteristics. First, they can take as subjects either physical objects, such as a stone, or things like the impact of a stone or the weight of a stone, or things not easily categorized, like the sun. (The sun that rises in the midst of clouds, is strong at noon, and feels barely warm in the evening, is no ordinary physical object.) Second, these verbs have both transitive and absolute uses which are systematically related: when the wind breaks a branch, the branch breaks; when it moves a leaf, the leaf moves; when the fire softens the wax, the wax softens. Examples of verbs with these characteristics include:

> *move, start, stop, lift, drop,*
> *bend, straighten, twist, break, tear,*
> *warm, cool, soften, harden,*
> *open, close, fill, empty*

All of these kinds of action of one inanimate thing on another can be analyzed in terms of the concept of an effect; more precisely in terms of two concepts of effect, one corresponding to the transitive and the other to the absolute use. As an example of the former, it may be that the effect that the wind has on the branch is to bend the branch. The wind might have a similar effect on other things, other things a similar effect on the branch—or a different effect on it, in that they broke the branch, or dried it out. As an example of the latter concept of an effect, the effect produced in the branch is that it bends, or breaks, or dries out. The one concept can be analysed in terms of the other. To bend a branch is to *make* the branch bend, or to *cause* it to bend, or to *produce* in it a bending. When the fire softens the wax, in the first sense the effect it *has* on the wax is to soften it, i.e., to make it go soft; in the second sense the effect it *produces* in the wax is that the wax softens, i.e., goes soft. As a dictum: some effects are to cause something to occur; some effects are caused to occur.

Actually, I think 'make' and 'produce' are more at home in these contexts than 'cause' and more instructive about the nature of effects. That is partly because 'cause' has many other uses besides that in 'cause something to do something', and in those uses it need have nothing to do with effects. The source of its greater range is that it embodies a concept which is primarily explanatory rather than physically descriptive.

2.3 MODES OF OPERATION

The selected concepts of inanimate action have two kinds of simplicity. The one, less remarkable, is that they contain neither reference to, nor restriction on, the agents which can fill the role of subject. The other, more interesting, is that they similarly ignore the way in which the agent produces the effect it does produce. The availability of the same verb for absolute as well as transitive uses is due to the fact that the concept is pure of any reference to how the agent operates; these are concepts of somehow-or-other producing a given effect. So whether the wind breaks the branch, or a falling tree breaks it, it gets broken. One can add, by the wind, by the tree, and in this way or in that, assigning the effect to one or the other agency, operating in one or another fashion. But specification of the effect produced is independent of specification of the subject, and even a complete statement of what produced what effects in what need not say anything about how.

Compare some kinds of inanimate action which lie outside the selected group, but adjacent to it. Among the ways of moving something are carrying it, throwing it, dragging it. Each concept combines the effect produced, that of motion, with some more or less general indication of how the agent did it, as that the water was under and supporting the log it carried, or that the log was ahead of and somehow attached to the seaweed it was dragging. The famous pair, pushing and pulling, deserve a certain pre-eminence in the description of action; their generality and abstractness can be appreciated through that of the technical concepts most closely related to them which are used in elementary mechanics.

Reflecting on the things so far reviewed which can be done by inanimate objects, I venture the generalization about any concept which is to be that of a kind of inanimate action, that the concept must contain the concept of producing some effect, and can, but need not, contain the concept of some mode of operation of the agent. The group of concepts originally selected seem to be the purest cases of inanimate action.

Although the concept of the inanimate producing of a given effect need contain nothing about any given mode of operation on the part of the agent, it is necessary that there be some mode of operation or other, and the question of how the agent produced the effect always applies. This is a consequence of the fact, which will call for further study later (4.9), that attributability of an effect to an agent is grounded on its attributability to an event which consists of the agent's doing something.

2.4 INANIMATE MOTION AND CHANGE

Inanimate action, which I have analysed as the producing of effects in other things, does not exhaust the range of things that an inanimate thing can do. Obviously a stone or the sun can simply move or change in some way. Aristotle was able to speak of change (*metabole*) in a very general sense, to distinguish motion (*kinesis*) as a kind of change, and among kinds of motion to distinguish local motion (*phora*) as change of place. English does not provide us with any single term for the category I have in mind, and it would be unhelpful to stretch a familiar word. If we are to confine ourselves to the things which inanimate things can be said to do, and if we are to avoid violence to English terms, it will be more accurate to speak of motion (including motion from one place to another, rotary and other stationary motion, and motion consisting in motion of parts), and of change (including change in size and shape, and change in other properties). We need not assume either that motion and change, in our terminology, are exclusive, or that either contains the other.

Not only do motion and change together constitute an obvious and familiar category of things which an inanimate thing can do, but this category is fundamental to the analysis of the producing of effects. The effect produced in a thing is typically an instance of that thing exhibiting some pure change or motion; and in cases where the effect consists in that thing acting on some third thing, it always at least includes some change or motion. At the other end of the relation, to say that an agent has a mode of operation is to say that it produces an effect *by* doing something else. This subsidiary thing which it does can be a case of action, as when a rope cracks a branch *by* bending it, or the sun evaporates water *by* heating it. But it need not be action; it can be sheer change or motion, as when water washes stones by flowing over them. When it *is* action, we can again look for the mode of operation, until we reach pure change or motion. So the concept of the effect produced, and that of the mode of operation of the agent, both involve change or motion. But change and motion do not involve either being an effect or producing an effect.

A Humean analysis of the producing of effects by one thing in another thing will isolate two events which are changes or movements, one on the part of the agent and the other on the part of the thing acted on, and will proceed to the constant conjunction of events of these two kinds. The Humean problem of what more there is to the necessary connexions between events at least overlaps with the problem of what more there is to the producing of effects, besides the constant conjunction of the mode of operation of the agent with the appearance of the effect in the thing acted on. At any rate, it is evident that the producing of effects belongs on a more complex level of analysis, on which enter, along with motion and change, such things as constant conjunction and the inferability of the occurrence of one event from the occurrence of another.

It is a central feature of the inanimate producing of effects that we can ask *how* it is done, in the sense of asking for the mode of operation. By contrast, inanimate change and motion do not admit of this question. The inapplicability of the question is evident from the senses in which we can and cannot ask *how*. We often ask how things moved or changed, meaning *in what manner*; we ask for a description. We can sometimes ask how, meaning *by doing what other things*, where the answer analyses into its parts a complex thing done. How, for example, does the cloud become mushroom-shaped? Is it by shooting straight to its height, then spilling over to all sides from the top? What we cannot in general ask is how a thing moved or changed, where we mean *by doing what other things*, and where the relation between doing those things and doing the original thing *thereby* done depends on a causal connexion. When the sun rises, or the tree-branch stirs, or the rain-water drips, the question of how it does it, in this sense, does not apply.

Suppose we add together the categories of inanimate action and of inanimate motion or change. We then have a category of things which an inanimate thing can do, encompassing any case in which such a thing either moves or changes or acts on something else. This category I believe to be nameless but familiar. Everyone agrees that the sheer category of things which an inanimate thing can do is too wide to be of philosophical interest, since it includes everything for which there is an active verb of which an inanimate thing can intelligibly be made the subject. There is nevertheless a habit of stressing the verb 'do' and treating it as though it were then capable of identifying a narrower category which is of interest. Thus if a stone lies on the ground, it doesn't *do* anything, even though 'lie' is an active verb. What is it for an inanimate thing to *do* something in this sense? I suggest that it is for it either to move or to change or to act on something else, or to do something which is a mixture of these.

2.5 MY ACCESS TO THE PRODUCING OF EFFECTS

The stage being set for human participation, the human actor may be carried on stage in his sleep, and roused. He will find himself in the midst of the action. Until his entrance, there is no distinction between his point of view and that of a spectator; the preceding stage directions have belonged to the area of discourse for which the distinction is not drawn, and their content is now available from either point of view.

My current enterprise is to adopt the point of view of the agent, and to examine from that point of view his participation in what is going on. For this purpose I am surveying the range of possible members of the category of things which it makes sense to consider doing. We need both to identify sub-classes of this category and to find which types are in various ways nuclear or peripheral. In search of such types we have turned to notice the doings of inanimate agents, and we must now consider the yield from the point of view of the agent. The class of things which I can be said in various senses to do is of course very wide. What is relevant here is the narrower class of things which can intelligibly find a place in the *question of whether to do them*.

Let us begin with the pure cases of natural action. For anything of this kind that stones and water can do, I can frame the question of whether to do it. I may not be physically able to do it, but it makes sense for me to wonder whether I could find some way to do it. If I can use one of these verbs at all, I can use it with myself as subject. This substitutability for other agents is direct: from my point of view, as an agent for whom arise various questions of what to do, there can arise the pure question of whether to produce a given effect in a given thing. The question of whether to break a branch is not analysable as the question of whether to move my body in such a way that the effect of its motion shall be to break the branch. It is logically possible that I should consider whether to break the branch, and decide to do it, and do it, without so much as knowing what movements of my body are involved, somewhat as I can consider moving my body without considering the inner workings of nerve and muscle. In doing things to something else, deliberation can deal directly with the effect to be somehow-or-other produced, and no further ideas need be involved in the concept of the thing to be done.

My substitutability for natural agents is *in principle* unbounded. I can in principle conceive of stepping into the role of any inanimate agent at any time.

There are two kinds of limitation on this principle of my general access to the field of natural action. First, there is of course no predicting *a priori* what limitations there are on the physical ability of given agents to produce given effects. Like the wind, I may not be strong enough to push down a tree, and where I am unable to do something, the question of whether to do it does not arise. It makes sense to frame the question, and it would make sense to consider it in other possible circumstances, but it does not make sense to raise it in these actual circumstances. Second, when we include kinds of natural action which are not pure, we must recognize certain general impossibilities. For A to *float* B, in one sense, A must not merely raise B, but also, being a liquid, must have B partly immersed in it. That particular agents as identified on particular occasions should answer to this specification may be a logical impossibility, or a physical impossibility, or just contrary to fact. To say that the agent acted in this way on B may accordingly become unintelligible in various ways; nor may it be easy to decide exactly what type of impossibility is in question. But at any rate the pattern of incompatibilities bears no essential relation to the contrast between inanimate and human action. The sun cannot wash a stone clean but the sea can. Neither of them can kick a stone in the air, but a horse and I can. Neither I nor the horse nor the sea can shine all afternoon.

The general question of my repertory of modes of operation will be the next to come up. But setting aside those concepts which by definition include a mode of operation, and keeping to pure action, we can say that my mode of operation, and in particular the specific role of my body, is not part of the concept of my producing any given effect. The concept of producing a given effect, which in the realm of natural action is evidently pure of any reference to specific modes of operation, preserves this purity when it occurs within my deliberation as an agent.

2.6 MY PARTICIPATION IN MOTION AND CHANGE

We have now seen that the producing of effects in other things comes, in principle, within the sphere of my deliberation. It is also obvious that the question of the mode of operation in the producing of an effect can have application in my case. For example, I can ask how to produce a given effect, where this is the thing I want to achieve, and I can find a solution to this practical problem in the doing of some second thing, *by* doing which I produce the desired effect. The presumption might seem to be that the question of how I produce any given effect is always applicable, and always answerable. If so, what are my modes of operation? Do we find in them a new type of thing the doing of which I can deliberate about, just as moving-or-changing constitutes a second type of thing an inanimate thing can do?

Let us first notice that, as a matter of fact, there are things which I can deliberate about, the doing of which is a case of pure moving or changing on my part—even though the repertory of such things proves to be curiously limited. Then, in the following section, let us examine two opposite theoretical temptations to generalize about my basic modes of operation. It will appear that these are not necessarily kinds of pure moving or changing, and are not necessarily kinds of producing of effects, but can be either, and can be mixed.

Once again we are interested not in the whole class of things which *a*) do not involve the producing of an effect and which *b*) I can intelligibly be said to do, but only in the sub-class of these which *c*) can intelligibly find a place in the question of whether to do them. This sub-class is not much narrower; most of the things I can do at all I logically could deliberate about. But many of these questions cannot in fact arise; I cannot deliberate about whether to become hotter or to turn brown. It will therefore become interesting to consider which of these things *d*) can actually be deliberated about. The things which fall in the narrowest class are typically ways of moving: to crouch or get up, approach a thing or go away from it, walk or run, raise my arm or straighten my knee. Generally speaking, in the ways in which an inanimate object can move, I can move, and I can deliberate about whether to move. The limitations which attach to application of this general rule are those already noticed for modes of operation in general: I may lack the strength; I cannot flow because I am not a liquid; and a liquid cannot raise its arm because it has no arm. But there is no essential connexion between these limitations and the contrast between inanimate doing and human doing.

There is a curious fact about the noun 'action', the significance of which is hard to assess. If there is some thing which I can consider doing, and which is pure motion or change without the producing of an effect, then my doing of it can count as action, even though the doing of this same thing by an inanimate object would not count as action. Once I have jumped from an airplane, my moving towards the ground is no more an action of mine than the falling of a bomb is an action of the bomb's. However, when I have noticed a squirrel in a tree, my moving towards the tree is an action of mine. Part of the reason seems to be that moving towards the tree is one of the things about which the question of whether to do it arose for me in that situation. It appears that the differentia, within inanimate doing, of inanimate action is not the same as the differentia, within human doing, of human action. Both inanimate things and persons can exhibit sheer motion or change, and both can produce effects in other things. An inanimate thing becomes an agent, and what it does becomes an instance of action, only in the latter case of producing an effect. A person becomes an agent, and what he does becomes an instance of action, in either case, but only when the thing done is such that the person, not actually considers, but at least can consider, whether to do it or not. For now the contrast can be left as a raw linguistic datum; an explanation of it will be attempted in Chapter 4.

The notion of a human action that does not involve the agent's producing an effect in anything else is easy to formulate, but examples are not plentiful. This is roughly the region of locomotion and sheer bodily movement. We must allow our examples to include spatial relations and pushings and pullings such as are logically involved in walking, in leaning against a tree, or even in raising one's arm; to select cases pure of such elements would confine us to an odd residue of things like opening one's eyes or doubling up and straightening. But we must exclude breathing and eating, and manipulations of any kind, since these do logically involve producing effects in other things. The resulting class of things has a very artificial air. In short, we are in practice strikingly indifferent to any distinction between producing effects and moving or changing. The typical things we do, like drinking a cup of coffee, writing, driving down town, or voting for a proposal, are complex mixtures of moving, producing effects, and many other things as well.

However, the producing of effects is a concept of great philosophical interest. Preoccupation with it suggests two opposite theories

about a person's basic modes of operation, both false, and these I
now examine.

2.7 MY BASIC MODES OF OPERATION

Where A is said to do y, let us consider those cases in which y is the
producing of some given effect in another thing B. Then we can ask
how A does y, i.e., how A produces this effect in B. Let x be some
thing *by* doing which A does y. Where A in this sense does y *by*
doing x, I have spoken of the doing of x as A's mode of operation in
doing y.

In the terms of this schema, one is tempted to suppose that in
every instance in which A produces an effect in B, one can find A's
mode of operation. And in fact as long as A is an inanimate object
this rule seems to hold good. I pointed out in 2.4 that the analysis
of inanimate action depends on the concept of pure motion and
change, in the following way. The mode of operation of A can either
be itself the producing of an effect, or it can be sheer motion or
change. In the former case, it must be possible, by asking how in
turn this effect is produced, to follow up a chain of modes of operation to a primary one which is sheer motion or change on the part
of A. When A's doing x falls in this category, there is no further
thing *by* doing which, in this sense, A does x. In other words, A has
no mode of operation in doing x. In general, where A has no mode
of operation in doing x, the doing of x can be called A's *basic* mode
of operation in producing the original effect.

Now let A be myself, and let the doing of y be my producing of
some effect in B, where it makes sense for me to frame the question
of whether or not to do y. In cases where I do y *by* doing x, the
doing of x will be my mode of operation, and there is again the
possibility of a chain. At the end of the chain, where there is nothing
by doing which I do x, the doing of x will be my basic mode of
operation in producing the original effect in B.

What can be said about my basic modes of operation? There is
a strong temptation to transfer to my own case expectations derived from the structure of inanimate action. It might seem that
among the things I can deliberate about we must be able to locate

the class of my basic modes of operation, and that these too must consist entirely in sheer moving or changing on my part. For example, I may fill the tank by pumping water, and I may pump the water by working the pump handle up and down, and I may move the handle by grasping it and moving my arm up and down. In the sheer motion of my arm we reach my basic mode of operation in filling the tank. The theory is that all my basic modes of operation are similarly cases of pure moving or changing.

In fact this parallel with inanimate action breaks down. There are things about which I deliberate, which consist in producing an effect in other things, and which I do not do *by* doing anything else whatever. For example, suppose that I clear the dust off my copy of the *De Anima* by blowing on it. My mode of operation in producing this motion of the dust is blowing. Blowing consists here in producing a stream of air by pursing my lips and at the same time breathing sharply out. But breathing out is itself making air stream out of me. By what mode of operation do I produce this effect on the air? Strictly speaking, by none whatever. There is nothing else *by doing which* I breathe; I simply can and do breathe in and out, slowly or sharply, at will. It is something I can do, but not something I know how to do.

This is not merely a case in which I produce an effect without knowing my mode of operation; I produce it without, myself, having a mode of operation. In place of the further thing I do, *by* doing which I produce an effect, there is a gap.

As far as the air is concerned, the motion of which is produced by *something* which goes on, the gap is filled by my body and its parts. (One needs no tools, if one has servants to do the work.) When I produce this effect my lungs contract, and by contracting they produce the effect for me, though I may well be unaware of the fact. So I produce the effect by my lungs producing the effect. The syntax embodies a problem, as my body embodies me.

Perhaps the motion of my body or its parts is my mode of operation. This would be, in the case where my producing of effects is opaque to me, to speak of a mode of operation which was mine but was hidden from me. I would claim as mine those things my body does, below the opaque surface of my deliberation, which are in fact my body's mode of operation in its producing of the effect. For it is true both that I produce the effect and that my body, or part of it, produces this same effect. How else would I be able to do it? But when my lungs contract, it is simply incorrect to say that *I* do this at all; the only agents involved, whose motion is in question, are my lungs. I neither contract, nor contract my lungs—I breathe. My lungs do not breathe; they contract and force the air out. Certainly I have some kind of claim on what they do. I have more than squatter's rights in my own body. But to call the motion of my lungs *my* mode of operation is to miss the categorical distinction between me and my body, and to lose hope of understanding what it is to be embodied.

In concession to the evident temptation to say that whether I know it or not I do contract my lungs, we should add qualifications. We must stand by our denial that it is correct to say straightforwardly and without qualification that in this case I contract my lungs. But how shall we deal with the fact that given adequate qualification and an adequate context of explanations we can unmisleadingly say at least that the contraction of my lungs is something which I make happen when I breathe? Formally the answer is that there exists a stretched sense of 'make happen', and similar terms, in which I do make this happen; the dependence on special context and qualifications is the symptom of the sense being stretched, and the relegation of the objection to the category of 'true only in a stretched sense' is the defence of my simple denial above. This must suffice for the moment. But the stretched sense, we are about to see, forms the basis of the alternative theory to be examined next, and will call for further discussion. Full satisfaction about the stretched sense will only be available from the theory of attributability to be developed in the final chapter.

We must therefore reject the suggestion that, if we begin from my producing of effects and inquire into my modes of operation, we will be led along the chains to a category of basic modes of operation, all of which will consist in pure moving or changing on my part. The most elemental thing I do may itself be the producing of an effect, and for that I may have no mode of operation at all.

We have found an exception to the rule that where A produces an effect in B, there must be some moving or changing which A does by which it produces the effect. The peculiarities of the exception are such that the exception proves more about the exception than about the rule. In the human agent, straightforward attributability of the effect to him opens the possibility of attributing it to something he does; then, in the case examined, this possibility fails us. But the very possibility of attributing to him a physical effect depends throughout on the simultaneous possibility of attributing the same effect to something his body does. At the point where the person's role in the chain of modes of operation shows a gap, we see through the gap to the constant presence of his body and the things it does. Then we realize that even in those cases in which he does *y* by himself doing *x*, his doing of *x* could not have achieved the production of the effect unless it too had had as one of its aspects his body's moving or changing and thereby acting on the thing affected. The series which remains complete is the series of physical interactions. The person's participation in the producing of effects disappears no more mysteriously than it enters.

We have seen not only that my deliberation can deal directly with an effect to be somehow-or-other produced but that it can deal with the producing of an effect in the producing of which I have no mode of operation at all. There being no necessity for pure moving or changing by me, in order for me to have access to the producing of effects, let us consider the opposite theoretical temptation, which is to suppose that there is no possibility of pure moving and changing by me within the sphere of my deliberation. Perhaps my own analysis of what I do and how I do it must always stop short at a producing-of-an-effect which is opaque to me, in the sense that I do not do it by doing anything else. Such a theory, to gain as much as initial plausibility, must analyse the apparent cases of pure moving as really being, after all, the producing of effects. It happens that there are independent motives for analyses that would have this consequence, in particular for the theory that the concept of human action is analysable in terms of the producing of effects.

Consider the event which consists in a person stepping out of his car. This is an action; but suppose that we construct as full an account of what happens as we can without reporting any action. Then we have a description of movements of parts of his body, forces exerted by muscles, motion and orientation of his body as a whole, and so on. Now then, it is argued, in stepping out of his car the person in question makes all this happen. Similarly he makes happen the thousands of discharges which occur in his motor neurones. But since some externally observable involvement of the body is essential to any case of human action, it is also essential that the agent make some such physical events happen. Consequently, any human action must be partly analysable in terms of the producing of effects in one's own body.

This theory might be combined with a theory of volitions and perhaps of mind–body interaction, according to which one produced the effects in one's body *by willing*. But to take such a line is rather to reinstate the demand for a basic mode of operation which is pure motion or change, with the difference that this motion or change is now mental, and the mode of operation is now related to the production of the effect as a mental event producing a physical event. Given the familiar objections to such a view, it is more interesting to stay with the simple rejection of *any* basic mode of operation which consists of sheer moving or changing.

We are granting throughout that on the face of it I do simply move: I get out of the car, I nod, smile, walk, bend over, extend my hand. It is therefore enough if we can disarm the reasons given for saying that these things I do must after all be analysed as the producing of an effect.

We must not complain that by the offered analysis the things my body does are attributable to *me*, without being attributable to anything I do, and that this is an unintelligible kind of attribution. For this is precisely the kind of attribution we have just defended in arguing that my basic mode of operation can be itself the producing of an effect on something else. The location of the produced physical effect inside rather than outside my body does not by itself present a new difficulty. For just as in the one case the needed physical agent is supplied by my body itself, so in the other case the needed physical agent can be supplied somewhere in the internal mechanism of my body.

The trouble lies rather in a subtle but systematic shift from the straightforward sense in which I make things happen to that stretched sense we noticed above. The argument for the analysis of action just outlined, and for the entailed theory that my basic modes of operation must all be producing of effects, began by constructing a description of the agent's bodily movement in terms which attributed nothing to him. Then, it said, he makes all this happen. But in the straightforward sense which is relevant here, it is simply not true that he makes it happen. It is plausible to say that he does only because the argument has assembled some of the facts in the light of which we can be induced to admit that 'well, yes, in a sense he makes it happen, but . . .'. I take it to be characteristic of stretched senses that they occur when some but not all of the conditions are satisfied for use of the term in the unstretched sense. The concessive use of the term acknowledges the satisfied conditions; the attendant 'but' warns against the implication that the rest of the conditions are also satisfied. The context of discrimination and qualification is the force which stretches the use of the term; beyond the reach of this force and for purposes of further argument, the term contracts to its standard application, and the assertions in which it occurs are untrue. In any case, whether we allow the assertions in a stretched sense, or deny them in a standard sense, we refuse to allow certain implications of the standard assertion.

Some of the implications needing denial in this case are easy to see, others are more controversial. One fairly obvious one, which is useful as a touchstone of the difference in sense, is this. The straightforward assertion that I make something happen implies that I know that it happens; the corresponding assertion in the stretched sense does not. The argument under criticism abandons the standard sense in which a man might be said to make his legs move; the mark of this abandonment is the unlimited freedom with which we can go on in the new sense to say that he makes happen the functioning of mechanisms in his body of whose existence he is ignorant.

By reflecting on such points, we can recognize a relation between two things. One is the domain of standard application of terms like 'make happen', and the other is the domain of things about which the agent can deliberate on any particular occasion. For example, consider the contraction of a particular muscle which the agent in the stretched sense makes happen, but without knowing that it happens. It seems that the same consideration which require us to deny that in the standard sense the agent makes this happen at all, also show that on this occasion he could not deliberate about whether to make it happen. Curiously enough, it may well be the case that, from the point of view of the agent, the question of whether or not to make it happen did arise, but the agent did not know that the question arose, and so could not deliberate about it. Suppose we inform the agent that, every time he raises his arm, a certain muscle contracts. It will now be possible for his doctor to ask him to make that muscle contract, and for him, having decided to oblige the doctor, to make it contract by raising his arm. But the information we have supplied to him is the indispensable basis both of bringing the contraction of the muscle within the sphere of his deliberation and of saying, without qualification and yet truly, that he made the muscle contract.

These considerations I offer as conceptual data, although I would agree that as data go they are not the rawest or the firmest imaginable. My own confidence in them is due to the explanation of them that would be provided by the theory of the standard sense of action words to be developed in 4.11 and related sections. According to that theory, making something occur will be unqualifiedly a case of human action only if the explanation of the occurrence refers at some point to the settling of the agent's question of whether to make that thing occur. The connexion between the standard sense of 'make happen' and the possibility of deliberation would then be a consequence of the analysis of the concept of human action. For present purposes, it is enough if I have shown that, for whatever reason, the occurrence or the physical indispensability of events in the body is not a sufficient ground for holding that the agent makes these events happen. Modes of operation and basic modes of operation, being definable in terms of the standard language of action, cannot be circumscribed on such grounds. I conclude that there is no reason to deny that my basic modes of operation may include sheer motion or change.

Neither theory about my basic modes of operation holds up. There is no *a priori* requirement either that they consist of pure moving or changing by me, or that they consist of my producing of an effect, and in fact they happen to be sometimes the one and sometimes the other. This result shows something about the independence of two systems of concepts. Causes and effects, and in particular modes of operation and effects produced, are analysable on fundamentally Humean lines in ways determined largely by straightforward physical applications of the concepts. On the other hand, the things which can be deliberated about are analysable into their own elements. These are often drawn from the realm of physical transactions in which we participate through the participation of our bodies. But the points of contact between the two analyses, and in particular any correspondances between primitive elements in the one and primitive elements in the other, are a contingent matter. When the human agent wakes in the midst of natural action, what he wakes up to is the fact that he just does, and therefore can, breathe, eat, run, pick things up, and throw them. Deliberation is a beam of light which cuts this or that section through the events in which he is involved, but it need not pick out the same things as we can by analysing and re-sorting what he does into moving or changing and producing effects.[2]

2.8 MY BODY'S REPERTORY

We have identified that class of things which I can consider doing which are pure moving or changing on my part, and we have looked at the relation, within the structure of my deliberation, between them and my producing of effects. Let us return to the question of the range of members for the class. Why are they typically cases of locomotion and bodily movement, and what kinds of limit are there on membership? We cannot assume, for every member of the class, that the doing of it would be a case of action. It might belong to a kind of mental doing which had no current externally observable aspect, and such doing does not count as action (see 2.1). Let us therefore be content with a less ambitious question, about action alone. In the field of *action* which consists of pure moving or changing by me, what is there for me to do?

The restriction on the question suggests the answer. In whatever sense my body's bending over supplies the content of my bending

2 Compare Austin Farrer, *The Freedom of the Will* (London : A. and C. Black, 1958), Chaps. 2 and 3.

over, it is the moving or changing of my body which supplies the content of my moving or changing. We do not need a full account of the difference between my bending over and my body's bending over in order to say at least that the former logically involves the latter; and that the latter, in that aspect by which my sense organs enable me to identify it, is precisely what presents itself to my point of view as an agent in the question of whether to bend over. What then can my body do?

As physical objects go, my body has an extraordinary repertory. Aside from all the ways it can move, it can grow and regenerate parts, it can change in size and weight, it can change colour in several ways, it can alter in surface texture, in hardness and softness, in rigidity and flexibility, in temperature, in electrical resistance, and in distributions of these over its parts. But it is striking that many of these things do not count as things which *I* do at all, and of those that do count very few are things about which I can deliberate. The things over which, in the traditional phrase I 'have voluntary control', are almost entirely movements.

It seems clear that this kind of limitation on the things I can consider doing is a matter of empirical fact. Our somewhat fumbling grasp in practice of what we can and cannot do with our bodies is the fruit of experience. The characteristic pattern of human ability and inability is ultimately due to the biological evolution of our nervous systems, which in this respect has favoured the striped muscles.

It follows that my modes of operation in producing effects might have been radically different. In fact I rely heavily on pushing and pulling. I might have exploited more fully my thermal radiation; it has made the sun influential, while I dispense it to no great purpose. My body has chemical modes of operation on my food, and I might have worked chiefly by extending my pseudopodia to bring external objects into the range of chemical action about which I could deliberate. There are probably very general physical facts which account for the pre-eminence of motion, collision, and pushing and pulling at the human scale of magnitude, and for the specialization of efferent nerves to literally motor functions. Had these facts been otherwise, then, instead of taking steps, breaking down obstacles, and building machines, I might have shifted my magnetic field, melted food, and synthesized substances like a plant that knew what it was doing. I might have had a life of action which accomplished as much in the world, with less noise.

But on this view it should be an empirical fact that I cannot deliberate about whether to turn brown, or whether to rise in temperature, or whether to beat my heart. Surely the question of whether to do any of these things does not make sense. How is the unintelligibility of the question to be accounted for by physiological facts?

Two things might be meant by a question making sense. It is one thing for a form of words to have a meaning, in that there can be occasions on which one can ask a question by using this form of words. In that case it makes sense to *frame* the question; the question is such that it *can* arise. It is another thing for a question actually to arise, in that some occasion or class of occasions is in fact such that the use of the form of words does result in a successful linguistic act. The question of whether to write to the King of France makes sense, in that the form of words has a meaning; it makes sense to frame the question. But the question does not in fact arise on any present occasion.

Among the circumstances which prevent meaningful questions of what to do from arising is physical inability to do the thing in question. The question of whether to carry a 200 lb. sack on one's shoulders makes perfect sense, but for many people does not arise. The same can be said for such things as standing on two fingers and holding one's breath for ten minutes. In this type of case, the limit of ability is set by the physiological impossibility of the required events occurring within the body; I cannot because my body cannot. It is characteristic that the performance lies on a scale some region of which I can encompass, and that in the absence of knowledge that the performance lies beyond one's ability, an attempt is possible.

In the case of turning brown, or rising in temperature, the presupposition which fails is analogous to that of physical ability, and may be expressed in the same form of words, but must be distinguished from it. Wishing to do either of these things, I may observe that I am unable to; I cannot do it. But both things are physiologically quite possible, and when, after a sunburn, I find myself turning brown, I cannot stop doing it; at the onset of fever, my temperature goes up and I cannot stop it going up. At the same time, the attempt to do either thing is out of the question. An instruction or request to turn brown, understood on the model of that simply to raise a hand, leaves me baffled. It is not that I cannot do it; I do it every year; it is rather that I cannot do it, when I am not doing it; and I cannot not do it, when I am doing it. In short, I cannot do it at will. It seems equivalent here to deny that I can do it at any given time; that I can do it at a randomly chosen time; that I can do it when I choose; that I can do it if I choose.

I have already asserted, speaking from the spectator's point of view, that the ability to raise my arm at will and the inability to change its colour at will are physiologically determined. It seems to be an empirical impossibility of a relatively sophisticated kind that I should be able at will to change my skin pigmentation. It cannot be known *a priori*, to the agent either, which of the ways of moving and changing of which his body is capable will provide him with things which he can do at will. How then does the agent discover this? A limit to his physical strength is something that he can discover in the attempt, by the pattern of his failures. But here the very attempt is baffled. Deprived of the taking of means, unacquainted with lesser degrees of the same kind of performance, the agent finds that the question arises or it does not. If it does not, there is no relevant attempt; and if it does, the presupposition to be tested must already be satisfied. However complicated the empirical basis of this presupposition, the agent seems to stumble on its presence or absence as on a simple datum.

The simplicity with which the fulfilment of the presupposition is given is in one respect easily accounted for. That I can do something at will is established by a single occasion on which I do do it and on which my doing of it is in fact an exercise of my ability to do it at will. Granting that there are in fact some things I can do, and some I cannot, the experience of actually doing the things I can do at will provides a voluntary spectrum of things I do, somewhat as visual experience provides a visible spectrum of colours.

This seems paradoxical because it appears that one of the conditions my doing must satisfy in order to be an exercise of my ability to do the thing at will is that I should know already that I have this ability. For unless I know this already, it seems that the bodily movement may come as a surprise to me, and it seems that whenever I exercise my capacity to do something at will, without misadventure, I am expecting that which does happen. But this last suggestion is simply false. It may well be that once I am familiar with my ability, it will then hold good in general that I am expecting what happens in any exercise of the ability. But there is no reason to insist that this holds for a first or early case. It is possible to have the ability to do something at will, and not to have exercised it or discovered that one has it. The look of delighted astonishment I have seen on the face of a child during his first four walking steps seems to me intelligibly diagnosed not merely as astonishment at having walked but also, in part, as astonishment at being able to walk at will.

But how can the first occasion be one on which I *do the thing at will*? Does not *this* imply that I am expecting what happens? The supposition implies nothing, because it is not well formed. 'At will' fits into the matrix 'I can ... do it' but not into 'I did it ...'. It has a similar force to that of 'if I choose', and 'I did it at will' makes no more sense than 'I did it if I choose'.

No doubt some psychological conditions must be satisfied by any action that is to be the first or any other exercise of an ability to do that thing at will. But what we have seen is that these do not include knowledge that one has the ability.

There is some residual mystery here, which I will explore further in 3.4 to 3.6. But we have run to ground, at least in one of its branches, the question of what things there are about which it makes sense to deliberate. In its most general statement, our enterprise has been to survey the possible members of the category of things about which it makes sense to frame the question of whether to do them. Having limited ourselves to action, and thereby excluded purely mental doing, we then selected the area of human action which mapped exactly to the area of inanimate action. As one inanimate thing can produce effects in another, and as it can move or change, so I can frame questions of whether to produce effects in other things, and whether to move or change in certain ways. Having explored some of the interrelations among these kinds of doing, we have encountered some features of the role of my body in the two classes of human actions. With respect to each of the two classes we have available to us a kind of reservoir of possible materials from which to draw instances for the category of things I can deliberate about. For the one, we have the range of effects which, as a matter of empirical fact, we find can be produced in things by other things. For the other, we have the range of ways in which, as a matter of empirical fact, we find our bodies can move or change. Whatever effect can be produced, and whatever ways my body can move or change, I can in principle frame a question of whether to produce the effect, and a question of whether to move or change in that way. In that sense of making sense, we have right there an account of the content of these two classes of things which fall within the category to be surveyed. But going on to consider which questions of what to do make sense in the further sense of sometimes arising, we have had to attend to further sets of empirical possibilities and impossibilities. Where I am physically unable by doing anything whatever to produce an effect in something else, the question of whether to do so lacks one of the presuppositions of its arising. A similar limitation holds for physical inabilities to move or change in particular ways. But in addition we have noticed for my moving and changing (and a similar condition will apply to that producing of effects for which I have no mode of operation) the condition that I just be able to do the thing at will. All these phenomena and all these limitations are discoverable from the point of view of the agent. So we have completed this part of the account of where the instances come from to supply the content of the category of things about which it makes sense to deliberate.

2.9 SOMATOKINESIS

The matter of my basic modes of operation has turned out to be doubly contingent. The things which I do, not *by* doing anything else, can consist either of producing an effect in something else or in sheer moving or changing; and among the ways in which I can move and change, I stumble on the things which I can and cannot do at will as on a series of brute facts. In this light the intelligibility of psychokinesis is a complex and instructive issue. Let us ignore the amateur Cartesianism with which parapsychologists burden their definitions of the term, and the oblique and jejune experiments with which they try to demonstrate the thing. Let us consider what ideas might sensibly be entertained and why there could or could not be such things, keeping to those conceptions on which psychokinesis will approximate to action rather than to the unforeseen consequence of conscious or unconscious mental events.

We are at any rate considering the producing of motion in another thing, and a robust example would be opening a door. As I approach the store exit, arms full of parcels, I fix my eyes on the door ... and open it. But of course we must not in setting up the example withhold the use of my arms, only to let me deliberately step on a treadle or walk by a photo-electric cell. In that case I might as well turn a crank or kick the door with my boot, since we have only a luxurious example of the ordinary producing of effects by means of the manipulation of intermediate physical objects. Whatever psychokinesis is to be, it must exclude the producing of the effect *by* pushing, pulling, manipulating, or otherwise using my body in order to act on other physical things. Then how do I open the door? At least two possibilities remain. One is that I have no way of opening the door, but just open it, as I have no way of opening my hand, but just open it. The other is that I open the door by doing something mental, such as conjuring up the visual image of the door open.

The first idea amounts to taking the concept of ordinary bodily movement as a starting point, and trying to reach psychokinesis by displacing the motion produced from my body to another physical object. From the point of view of the agent, such action is quite intelligible. As I wake up to the fact that I can open my hand at will, I could wake up to the fact that I can open the door at will. Indeed a friend of mine became quite excited for a few days when the local market introduced photo-electric doors. In the case of blowing, cited as the producing of an effect with no mode of operation, the motion of my breath is no more mediated or achieved than the opening of my hand. So if this specification of the concept is complete, psychokinesis in fact occurs. It is rather untypical, but its physical mechanism, in this case the lungs, is normally obvious. Such opening of doors at a distance does not occur, but if it did, its mechanism might be far from obvious. Such cases would approximate quite well to the kind of phenomenon which claims of psychokinesis have seemed to promise. It would be magic without magic art. Distance is so effective a guarantee of opaqueness of the mechanism that one can understand the original name of telekinesis.

It might be objected to this conception, on which psychokinesis occurs in familiar cases, and could but does not in fact occur in empirically strange cases, that its exclusion of a mechanism applies only from the point of view of the agent. Perhaps psychokinesis needs to be defined from the point of view of the spectator, to exclude not only my mode of operation, but also any mode of operation by any part of my body. When I just open the door, it will be psychokinesis only if the opening of the door is not causally explainable by reference to anything happening in my body, even to things unknown to me. Now, however, we have a conceptual marvel, and not merely an empirical one. The motion of the door must be a gross physical event with no physical cause at all, else it would be attributable to that cause and not to me. Had we stomach to go further, we would no doubt be driven to identify a mental event as cause, to be the basis of attributing the motion to me, and moreover a mental event for which a physical correlate or aspect was either lacking or else both present and correlated with but causally irrelevant to the motion of the door.

The second idea, according to which I open the door by doing something mental, encounters similar alternatives. From the point of view of the agent, it is quite conceivable that one should discover that it is possible to open doors by forming a sufficiently clear visual image or by cursing, purely in one's mind, in Arabic. Innocent subjects in psychology laboratories have in fact been charmed by their ability to swing a beam of light to one side just by imagining an animal. Once again, we can choose between an agent's conception on which psychokinesis occurs, but has not been shown to occur in any very impressive circumstances; and a spectator's conception on which the agent's ignorance of the bodily mechanism is replaced by an actual absence of bodily mechanism, and psychokinesis by definition involves physical events without physical causes.

For the time being I have regarded it as a *reductio ad absurdum* of the conception of a kind of action that it should involve the occurrence of physical events without physical causes. This consequence seems involved in attributing any physical effect to me without attributing it to some physical event in my body. As a matter of fact such an attribution is ruled out by the spectator's criteria for attributing a physical effect to me. That this is so is one way of restating the proposition that those actions of mine which consist of producing effects depend on the inanimate action of my body. In that sense, I am confined to somatokinesis.

2.10 THE NON-CONTINGENCY OF BEING EMBODIED

This chapter set out to find matter for a form of question. From the point of view of an agent, i.e., of a person for whom there can arise the question of whether or not to do things of various kinds, I have selected and examined a couple of kinds of action. The agent's own body has dominated the account, and to the extent that these are nuclear kinds of action it dominates the account of action. What I have done is to sketch the role of the body as the agent sees it, or sees through it, and then, where it seemed called for, to add a side view or a diagram from the point of view of the spectator. It is so familiar to us to think about action from a mixture of the two points of view that it has been something of an exercise to distinguish the point of view of the agent. Such a distillation of the pure point of view of the agent tends to generate the illusion that the agent's relation to his body is contingent. To show how this happens I now assemble some of the features of the agent's point of view that have come to light.

First, the category of individuals which is by definition correlative to the point of view of the agent, being the category of things about which it makes sense to frame the question of whether to do them, is extremely hospitable. Things to do can be mental or bodily, available to inanimate objects or only to people, done to other things or confined to oneself, simple or complex. Second, when we select the concept of producing an effect, we are taking over from inanimate action a concept which is pure of any specification of the mode of operation by which the effect is produced. Third, I can and actually do produce effects in other things not only without knowing my mode of operation, but sometimes without having any mode of operation at all. Fourth, in cases of sheer bodily movement, although there is no need to analyse them as producings of effects in my body, there is a close analogue to the absence of modes of operation in the fact that there is no application for the question of *how* I stand or walk or extend my hand; and I am typically ignorant of the bodily mechanism of what I do. Fifth, it is a raw datum for me which ways I can move or change at will, in the sense that by experience I stumble on what I can and cannot do. Sixth, by reflection on these points one can see that something one might wish to call psychokinesis (although it does not happen in empirically surprising cases) is quite intelligible as long as the absence of physical mechanism is defined only from the point of view of the agent.

Surely then, I happen to be the sort of agent which has a body, and which happens to work through its body in doing anything which affects the physical world at large; but I might have happened to be a disembodied agent, perhaps with power to work my will directly on any part of the physical world. Some have conceived of God as that agent to whom the physical universe stands as my body stands to me.

In resisting the temptation to regard my embodiment as contingent, I can operate on two different levels of argument. The more accessible of these is the only one I can attempt. It consists in recalling that the point of view of the agent is not an independent conceptual realm, but one of two possible points of view on the same thing; it proceeds by juxtaposing to the above account certain spectator's comments. First, we have observed that when I produce a physical effect in another thing directly, i.e., with no mode of operation, it is also the case that my body produces the same effect. Second, this is only a striking illustration of the general point that whenever I produce a physical effect, my body produces this effect. Third, when I just move, my body moves, and there is in fact a physiological mechanism which explains this motion. These points suggest the reflection, fourth, that the attribution of any physical effect either in or out of my body to *me*, without at the same time attributing it to physical events in my body, drives one to denying that the effect has a physical cause at all, since a cause wholly outside my body precludes attribution to me.

The spectator has now drawn attention to an impossibility, but one which turns upon criteria not yet discussed for the attribution of physical effects not to inanimate agents but to persons. The spectator's view of the agent's embodiment must wait for fuller development until the discussion of attributability in Chapter 4.

The other level of argument is the general discussion of the identity of persons; it could be approached by digging down to the presuppositions of the point of view of the agent. That is by definition the point of view of a person for whom certain questions arise. That any question of what to do should arise for me at all requires that I be able to identify myself, and the conditions for the self-identification of persons, if fully set out, would themselves establish my body at the centre of the account. But along these lines I have nothing to add to Strawson's discussion of the identity of persons.[3]

3 P. F. Strawson, *Individuals* (London : Methuen, 1959).

3 The origin of the idea of agency

On the face of it there are at least two kinds of action—inanimate and human. One can also identify two corresponding groups of familiar problems. Some problems recognizably turn upon the nature of inanimate action, natural causation, the relation of cause and effect, causation in science, or whatever it is called; some turn upon the nature of human action, the conduct of responsible agents, intentional action, or the will. The relation between the two kinds of action is both a problem in itself and, historically, a resource invoked for the analysis of either kind. Some writers have also worked with a conception of *true* agency, or productive power, or efficacy, not necessarily identified with either kind of action, or even exemplified by either kind; God as creator and agent, and perhaps sole true agent, has sometimes been the bearer of such a conception of action.

The most instructive over-simplification of this history is this extreme one: the problem about inanimate action is the problem of induction; the problem about human action is the problem of free-will. Difficulty about how scientific knowledge is possible has its main root in the logical contingency of every effect that is actually produced. Difficulty about how the will can be free has its main root in the empirical necessity of every effect that we actually produce.

In the empiricist tradition, the strategy on either problem is to seek out the basis in our experience of our knowledge of truths, and to seek out the origin in our experience of the ideas we have. Sometimes the search for the origin of ideas like action, agency, or production canvasses inanimate and human action non-commitally, as Locke does when he looks for the origin of the idea of power. Sometimes, as with Berkeley, action is the prerogative of persons, and the failure to find any such idea (in his sense) reduces natural causation to an illusion or confusion. Sometimes, as with Hume, the analysis begins and ends with causation in nature, encompassing human action as a special case. Under the heading of the search for agency in our experience I include all inquiries which seek the origin of the idea of agency, however variously conceived, either in the observation of nature or in the introspection of the agent. I take this to be the empiricist form of analysis of the concepts involved.

With respect to inanimate action, the empiricist's search typically addresses itself to the nature of that necessity with which the effect occurs. With respect to human action, it typically addresses itself to one or another putative brute fact of personal experience, such as the fact that I can produce effects in other things, the fact that I can move my body at will, or the fact that I can do anything at all at will. This chapter will treat both problems, and will try to show how the form of the empiricist's enquiry in each case vitiates his analysis at the last stage. His programme precludes an adequate account of the idea of necessary connexion, and an adequate account of the brute fact of being able to do things at will, for reasons which will prove to be at bottom the same.

3.2 ANTHROPOMORPHISM ABOUT CAUSATION

I have so far been occupied with an account of that kind of action for which there is such a thing as the point of view of the agent. It seemed to require a pretty full analysis of the point of view of the agent, and of the form and matter of the questions in terms of which this point of view is defined. It has been largely descriptive, but I have not concealed that the description itself seems to me to provide a *prima facie* case for one view of the relation between inanimate and human action. I have taken for granted the concept of inanimate action, as a species of natural causation, in order to use it in the analysis of human action. Other elements of the analysis may render human action unique, and problematic in additional ways, but the concept of inanimate action remains primitive in the analysis given. The central role of the body seems to me to imply the exploitation of this concept at the heart of the agent's conception of his own action. I now defend this *prima facie* order of logical primitiveness against the view that inanimate action itself can only be conceived on the basis of some reference to human action, and in fact anthropomorphically. Perhaps my analysis stands, but works only for the reason that when we invoke natural action we are looking in a mirror. Perhaps the concept of the natural producing of an effect supplies what we want only because we have already confusedly projected into nature the whole conceptual structure to be analysed.

In order to investigate this suggestion, we must distinguish among the forms it might take. I will argue first that the suggestion is plausible only if it refers to the anthropomorphic projection not of free action but of action under necessity. Then I will examine accounts by Kelsen and Collingwood which develop this second alternative.

In just what ways might I be conceiving anthropomorphically the production of an effect by an inanimate agent? First, I may project myself into either cause or effect. As I act, so I conceive inanimate agents to act; or as I am on occasion forced to do something, so I conceive that thing in which the effect is produced as being forced to do something. Second, from either end of the causal relation I may place at the other end either another person or an inanimate object. I may model the action of the wind either on my getting other people to do things or on my manipulation of sticks and stones; for the bending which is produced in the branch, I may look either to the occasions on which I am coerced by another person or to those on which, though no one coerces me, the situation forces me to act, the circumstances leaving me no alternative. A theory about the concept of inanimate action is not absolutely required to exploit these possibilities in a coherent pattern when it is representing the concept as itself incoherent. There is nevertheless a presumption in favour of the attempt. The coherence to be expected in the concept would vary with the accuracy and generality of that mode of understanding in which it functioned. But a modest standard will call for persons at both ends of the causal relation, since chains are possible. It will also require both persons to act under some kind of necessity.

For consider the implications of the alternative, that of projecting free action. Since the effect is that which is *made* to happen, only the cause can be conceived as acting freely; and further, it must not be obviously itself an effect. This conception is apt for sources of spontaneous or unpredictable activity, like the wind and the sea, and is then a form of polytheism. It does not domesticate well, either for the subsidiary transactions whereby the log moved by the sea in turn moves the pebbles which in turn make a noise, or for homely causal chains like those exploited in splitting wood or in picking up a chain. To conceive of the first billiard ball as acting in this way would be to forget both the cue and the second and third balls.

It is probably Berkeley who makes the clearest imputation of widespread anthropomorphic confusion of this kind. He makes it clear that he identifies agency with volition. Ideas are inert, and only spirits can be active. 'When we talk of unthinking agents, or of exciting ideas exclusive of volition, we only amuse ourselves with words.' [1]

He says that:

> When we perceive certain ideas of sense constantly followed by other ideas, and we know this is not of our doing, we forthwith attribute power and agency to the ideas themselves, and make one the cause of another, than which nothing can be more absurd and unintelligible. [2]

In *Siris*, having claimed Newton's agreement, he says that even Newton

> may perhaps sometimes be thought to forget himself, in his manner of speaking of physical agents, which in a strict sense are none at all; and in supposing real forces to exist in bodies, in which, to speak truly, attraction and repulsion should be considered only as tendencies or motions, that is, mere effects, and their laws as laws of motion. [3]

1 Berkeley, *The Principles of Human Knowledge*, sec. 28.

2 *Ibid.*, sec. 32.   3 Berkeley, *Siris*, sec. 246.

Berkeley is indeed at pains to 'assign the cause of this prejudice, and account for its obtaining in the world'.

> But why they should suppose the ideas of sense to be excited in us by things in their likeness, and not rather have recourse to spirit which alone can act, may be accounted for, first, because they were not aware of the repugnancy there is, as well in supposing things like unto our ideas existing without, as in attributing to them power or activity. Secondly, because the supreme spirit which excites those ideas in our minds, is not marked out and limited to our view by any particular finite collection of sensible ideas, as human agents are by their size, complexion, limbs, and motion. And thirdly because his operations are regular and uniform.[4]

But we must regard Berkeley as explaining not merely why people fail to recognize the action of God, but also how people can come to conceive of physical things as agents. His explanations of the latter seem inadequate to the degree of confusion which he has to impute to anyone who conceives of each physical agent as a free spirit. Perhaps because he is willing to believe the worst about ordinary conceptions, he does not notice how bad, according to his theory, these would have to be. What he does not notice, curiously, is that the anthropomorphic projection of free action achieves minimal coherence only in the limiting form exemplified in the philosophical doctrines of Berkeley himself. If, like Berkeley, or like Malebranche before him, one identifies agency with volition, one can deal with nature only as a whole: the agent whose action is visible in nature must not be part of it, but behind or above it, acting through every part of it.

It seems then that if we are to be anthropomorphic about inanimate action without being incredibly incoherent, both the thing which acts and the thing which is acted on must be thought of as persons; the action of the causal agent must itself be an effect; and the heart of our conception is thinking of the thing acted on as *forced* to do something, or as doing what it *must* do. The role of the cause can be variously thought of. It may be an act of coercion by the agent, who is himself coerced to commit it; nature then is an

4 Berkeley, *The Principles of Human Knowledge*, sec. 57.

up-to-date perfectly totalitarian state. It may be behaviour on the agent's part which, without coercing the second agent, puts him under need or necessity or deprives him of alternatives; say an economy of bare subsistence. It may be behaviour on the occasion of which the second agent is legally required to do what he does; say an old-fashioned autocracy. These alternatives of course require appropriate interpretations for the expressions 'forced' and 'must'.

But now the theory of anthropomorphic projection seems to provide a solution to a familiar problem. Is not this 'must', on some interpretation, just that residue of the concept of causation, after relations of invariable consequence and inferrability have been analysed out, which philosophers have sought under the heading of 'necessary connexion'? Grant that such events as the effect always do occur, and can be predicted. If we say that, in addition, the effect must occur, we are hankering after our animistic conception. As we become reconciled to finding no impression of sense, nothing in the phenomena, from which this further idea could be derived, we purge superstition from our view of nature.

Professor Hans Kelsen, for example, asserts that originally, and even now vestigially, we draw no distinction between human society and nature, and conceive of trees and stones as subject, like ourselves, to the government of a divine will. The order of the cosmos is that of obedience to divine law; under this order the explanation of effects draws upon a principle of retribution on which good or ill effects are proportioned to their causes; the necessity under which all things act is the inviolability of norms laid down by the transcendental will. As the scientific conception of causality gradually develops, the laws become the laws of nature, the principle of retribution becomes the law of universal causation, and the legal and moral requirement becomes metaphysical or logical necessity. Of the final disappearance of necessity from contemporary physical theory, which he regards as completing Hume's work, Kelsen says

> *Its significance lies in the fact that the notion of causality was stripped of its most important element with which it was still burdened as the heir of the principle of retribution: Αναγκη. This is necessity*

with which Διϰη, the goddess of retribution, punishes evildoers and at the same time keeps nature in its prescribed course.[5]

R. G. Collingwood's theory is empirically less elaborate but conceptually much clearer. He says

> The cause-effect terminology conveys an idea not only of one thing's leading to another but of one thing's forcing another to happen or exist; an idea of power or compulsion or constraint.
>
> From what impression, as Hume asks, is this idea derived? I answer, from impressions received in our social life, in the practical relations of man to man; specifically, from the impression of causing (in sense I) some other man to do something when, by argument or command or threat or the like, we place him in a situation in which he can only carry out his intentions by doing that thing; and conversely, from the impression of being caused to do something.[6]

Collingwood draws the radical conclusion about the concept: 'If the vocabulary of practical natural science were overhauled with a view to eliminating all traces of anthropomorphism, language about causes in sense II [the practical or "handle" sense] would disappear. . .' .[7] Even his sense III, belonging to the theoretical sciences of nature, is infected: 'Causal propositions in sense III are descriptions of relations between natural events in anthropomorphic terms.' [8]

He is led to this conclusion because he thinks that causation in Sense III involves something 'in the nature of compulsion'.[9] Even though that something is often called necessity 'the original sense of the word "necessary" is an historical sense according to which it is necessary for a person to act in a certain way. . .' .[10]

These accounts of Kelsen and Collingwood are typical of genetically minded conceptual analyses. The knights in shining armour return, claiming to have delivered us from barbaric ways of think-

5 Hans Kelsen, *Society and Nature* (London: Kegan Paul, Truber and Trench, 1946), p. 262.

6 R. G. Collingwood, *An Essay on Metaphysics* (Oxford: Clarendon Press, 1940), p. 309.

7 *Ibid.*, p. 311.   8 *Ibid.*, p. 322.

9 *Ibid.*, p. 321.   10 *Ibid.*, p. 320.

ing. They draw a map on which three margins, those of prehistory, of the child's conceptions, and of preliterate cultures, are marked 'Here be monsters'. Thanks to their vigilance against anthropomorphic survivals, we can inhabit the city of the rational in which causality is known to be analysable in terms of functional relations and temporal order.

Gratitude for such an analysis of causation suggests that it would be uncharitable to inspect the empirical claims implied. Anyway it seems generally agreed that the child's mental development shows a parallel with that of the race, in that both begin in animism and gradually achieve the level of positive science. On the other hand, scepticism is reasonable about any theory coming from the murky regions of prehistory, child psychology, and the anthropology of ideas. Furthermore, my impression of the constant reassertion of such views is that they are offered as though self-evident. If this attitude does not reflect the abundance and clarity of empirical evidence, it might reflect the complacency of the Enlightenment and of nineteenth-century rationalism.

Suspicion grows when one notices how widespread is the confusion between a) having a concept, as evidenced by mastery of performances requiring it and of words embodying it, and b) having an analysis of the concept, or an account of the words, or a theory of the thing they refer to, or a picture or explanation of it. In the case of things like pushing, pulling, lifting, falling, flowing, and striking, possession of the concepts belongs on the bottom level of understanding shared by any people to whom language is useful in hunting, cooking, eating, and fighting. Cosmology, mythology, tribal legend, and religious art belong on a level not merely of reflection but of relatively sophisticated and prolonged cultural development. To the extent that assumptions, or for that matter demonstrated principles, about cultural progress have been taken to imply development in the possession of these basic concepts, the inference has been fallacious. In *Society and Nature* Kelsen offers over 200 pages of empirical documentation without noticing its *prima facie* irrelevance to the second question, that of simple possession of the concepts. We seem left with some reconstructed etymologies covering late periods of prehistory, and some arguable interviews of children by Piaget. What onus of proof lies on these bits of evidence? Once again, if we are clear that the relevant topic is the ground-level possession of physical concepts, the presumption would seem to be that we and our ancestors and our primitive contemporaries and our children can see quite well what is going on in front of our eyes, and are able to think about the world in mundane ways. Given an explanation of thunder as a god throwing down his hammer in anger, one can dispute what it shows about a people's picture of the cosmos. But they evidently know that when a hammer falls it makes a noise.

I will not rush from *a priori* scepticism about one empirical theory to *a priori* adoption of its opposite. The point of airing the empirical issues is to force the analysis of our existing concepts to stand on its own feet. But the traffic back and forth between empirical theory and conceptual analysis has been heavier than that between empirical theory and empirical evidence; it testifies to a belief which I think is well founded that the two inquiries can illuminate each other. When one cannot satisfactorily complete the analysis of an existing concept, dismissal of the residue as a confusion raises the question of how this confusion arose, and the dismissal remains suspect until an answer is found. Conversely, available histories of confusion can suggest lines of analysis. Since it is idle to pretend that one's analysis is completely free from the influence of empirical beliefs, it is best to be clear about the alternatives.

In particular, the relations between the analyses of causation given by Hume, on the one hand, and by the de-anthropomorphizers, on the other, can be misunderstood. Kelsen and Collingwood both begin by accepting constant conjunction as a partial analysis of the ordinary concept, and go on to find a problem over necessary connexion, and in these respects they are Humean. The further reflection that they also conclude necessary connexion to be, in some sense, not really in the objects but in the mind, tends to obscure the fact that they regard Hume's account of necessary connexion as inadequate, and that this is the occasion of their appeal to anthropomorphism. Hume, however, expressly denies that necessary connexion, whatever else it involves, is a projection of notions peculiar to our own action. To his question about the impression from

which the idea of necessary connexion is derived, he could not accept Collingwood's answer. He explicitly refuses the suggestion: 'That we feel an energy, or power, in our own mind; and that having in this manner acquired the idea of power, we transfer that quality to matter.'
He says that

> *to convince us how fallacious this reasoning is, we need only consider,*
> *that the will being considered here as a cause, has no more a discover-*
> *able connexion with its effects, than any material cause has with its*
> *proper effect.*[11]

This remark treats only the Berkleian form of appeal to human volition, but he shows in the same passage that he does not think any relevant relation to be exemplified in human action which is not also attributed in a literal sense to inanimate things: 'In short the actions of the mind are, in this respect, the same with those of matter. We perceive only their constant conjunction; nor can we ever reason beyond it'. Mill follows Hume in this. In the *Logic* he says: 'Our will causes our bodily actions in the same sense, and no other, in which cold causes ice, or a spark causes an explosion of gunpowder'.[12] We could say that, depending on the agents and their mode of operation, there may be magnetic action, or chemical action, or mechanical action, or volitional action.

We can separate here the Hume–Mill account of the relation between volition and bodily movement, which is no doubt objectionable, from the denial that the concept of our own action provides any contribution to that of natural causation. It is this denial which is inconsistent with any attack on anthropomorphism. However, it is Hume's positive account which sets him most significantly at odds with Collingwood.

> *There is no internal impression, which has any relation to the present*
> *business, but that propensity, which custom produces, to pass from an*
> *object to the idea of its usual attendant. This therefore is the essence*

11 Hume, *A Treatise of Human Nature*, ed. L. A. Selby-Bigge (Oxford: Clarendon Press, 1896), Appendix, pp. 632–3.

12 J. S. Mill, *A System of Logic*, 8th ed. (London: Longmans Green, 1872), III, v, 11.

of necessity. Upon the whole, necessity is something, that exists in the mind, not in the objects. . . .[13]

Both men locate the impression in us rather than in the phenomena. But Hume's determination of the mind to pass from one object to another, and 'to conceive it in a stronger light upon account of that relation',[14] is not a feature of action or of volition, but rather of belief upon evidence—i.e., of inference. Hume draws on the intellectual operations of the mind. He finds there not a damaging parallel, but the actual source of the idea of necessity. For he rightly takes that necessity of effects which he is analysing to be a 'theoretical' rather than 'practical' necessity. Where Collingwood says that we anthropomorphically conceive of the effect as having conclusive reasons for occurring, Hume says that we have conclusive reasons for expecting it to occur.

I will now argue that Hume is right against Collingwood. For that purpose we will need to consider the distinction between the necessity which Hume sees to be involved in causation and the practical necessity which Collingwood has in mind. It is only when we come to analyse the former necessity that we part company with Hume in his pursuit of the impressions from which the idea of causation is derived. In the following section I will give my own account of necessity. Then in 3.8 I will return to locate the point at which his empiricist programme of analysis had to be abandoned.

3.3 PRACTICAL, LEGAL, MORAL AND CAUSAL NECESSITY

Any thesis to the effect that the concept of inanimate action involves an anthropomorphic projection of a necessity under which persons act implies, first, that the concept is found on analysis to include some concept of necessity, and second, that this concept of necessity has correct literal application to what persons do but not to what stones do. The burden of proof of the thesis lies in

13 Hume, *A Treatise of Human Nature*, p. 165.
14 *Ibid.*, p. 165.

identifying the necessity involved in inanimate action, or causation generally, and in showing that the application of the concept
so identified is limited to persons.

The concepts of inanimate action, of production of an effect, of
causation, and of making things do things, do indeed include some
concept of necessity. Suppose the usual billiard ball to strike
another and make it move. Part of what is involved in the *making*
is this: given that standard conditions obtain and given the
striking of the one by the other, we can say, according to the time
of the striking, either that the ball must have moved, or that it must
be moving, or that it must be about to move, or that it will necessarily move. A way of denying that one kind of event is the cause
of another is to say that even when the first kind occurs the second
does not necessarily occur. These uses of 'must' and 'necessarily'
express the relevant concept, which I think is the same as Hume's
'necessary connexion'. I will refer to it as the concept of causal
necessity.

We can take for granted the Humean conclusion that causal
necessity is not logical necessity (as it is commonly called), while
recognizing a classic temptation to identify the two. But beginning
from Hume's own positive account, the literature has made heavy
weather of the positive account of causal necessity. If necessity is
just logical necessity, it will follow that the putative concept is a
confusion. If there are exactly two kinds of necessity, say logical
and pragmatic, this may suggest that causal necessity is a displaced
and illegitimate application of either or even of both concepts. Ayer
for example says of Hume's theory of 'necessary connexion' that

> it does not at all account for the assumption that instances of B must
> always follow instances of A, as distinct from the assumption that
> they actually always have, and always will. How are we to explain
> this use of the word 'must'? The answer is, I think, that it is either
> a relic of animism, or else reveals an inclination to treat causal con-
> nexion as if it were a form of logical necessity. These two explana-
> tions are not, indeed, psychologically exclusive of one another.[15]

In general, any view which recognizes that causal necessity is *prima
facie* applicable with reference to events of any type and which

15 A. J. Ayer, *The Foundations of Empirical Knowledge* (London:
Macmillan, 1940), pp. 185–6.

holds that outside the sphere of concepts characteristic of an agent's deliberation there is only logical necessity, will be driven to conclude that the concept of causal necessity is incoherent. Antecedent despair over the coherence of the concept might encourage one to accept theories on which it is a displacement to inanimate things of a concept applicable to persons. Conversely, such a theory might encourage one to despair of the concept. But I believe that the main conceptual reason, as opposed to any empirical reasons, for accepting the anthropomorphism theory is just the difficulty of giving a clear account of a kind of necessity which shall be other than logical and yet at the same time 'theoretical' as opposed to 'practical'. Perhaps recent discussions of 'empirical possibility' and 'empirical necessity' have made it clear enough at least that there is a coherent concept of this kind; especially when one considers that the analysability of causal necessity in terms of logical necessity and other concepts, and in general the logical relations between causal and logical necessity, are a distinct issue from mere recognition of the concept. But at any rate I am not aware of other conceptual considerations lending substantial support to the anthropomorphism theory.

If there are none, the attractiveness of the theory will evaporate when exposed to an adequate general account of the various kinds of necessity. Here I can offer in that direction only some points about kinds of necessity which belong to the point of view of an agent, and about their structural dissimilarities to logical and causal necessity.

Consider the following cases. First, man finds that his only chance of survival is to hang on to an overturned boat and wait for help. Then he must hang on and wait. We could also say: (he finds it) necessary to hang on; he has to hang on. Of the past: (he knew) he must hang on; (it was) necessary for him to hang on; he had to hang on. Of the future (he will find that) he must; (it will be) necessary to; he will have to. In application to such a case these are roughly equivalent expressions. These uses of 'must', 'necessary', and 'have to' express a concept which I will refer to for now as practical necessity. I take this to be the use of 'necessary' which Collingwood thinks to be the original one.

Second, a bank teller is ordered at gun-point to hand over the cash in his drawer. Then he must hand it over. Of him too we could say that he finds it necessary to, or has to, and so for the other tenses. The action of the robber makes that of the teller a case of acting under compulsion. This is to say that the robber deliberately places the teller in a situation in which the teller shall know or think that the robber's intentions leave him no reasonable alternative to acting as he does. But I do not see that the source and basis of this necessity make any difference to the type of necessity, or are reflected in any difference in the use of 'must', 'necessary', or 'have to'. I accordingly regard acting under compulsion as a special case of acting under necessity in a sense exemplified by both the first and second cases.

Third, let the robber himself set down a note saying 'You must put all the bills from the drawer in a plain envelope etc.'. Or consider a father saying 'You must be home by ten o'clock', or a doctor 'You must take these every day for a full week'.

With this type of case compare, fourth, that of the wage earner required by law to file an income-tax return by a stated date. Then by law he must file a return. We could also say that he is not legally permitted not to, that legally he has to, that according to the law it is necessary for him to do it.

One might be tempted to assimilate the third and fourth types of case to the first two as further special cases of practical necessity. The robber, the parent, and the doctor are either threatening or warning of consequences in the light of which the agent may well agree that it is practically necessary for him to do as he is told; the sanctions of the law seem merely a regular system of placing people under practical necessity. However, in both types of case the 'must' occurs within the wording of the demand, instruction, prescription, rule, or law, and in each case obedience is presupposed rather than made the subject of discussion. The force of the 'must' is not primarily to draw attention, for a demand whose content is already determinate, to the necessity of performance, but rather to establish the content of the demand by the exclusion of alternatives from it or by the exclusion of exceptions to a rule being laid down. This is most clearly so in the legal case, where the things people are being told to do are authoritatively laid down in writing for all members of a certain class. Even the person who does not propose to file an income-tax return, and thinks no one will notice, can consistently admit that by law he must do it. For present purposes I will pass over the non-legal uses of 'must' in telling people to do things, select the use exemplified in this case, and refer to the concept expressed as that of legal necessity.

Finally, consider a man who is at pains to save money because he owes it; or who does not perform work or other obligations because his family is ill and needs him home; or who serves on a committee because a social problem seems to him pressing and neglected. At various points in stating or in summing up the moral considerations bearing on his action, we could say that he must repay a sum of money; that he must look after his family; that he must give some time to this problem. These are cases respectively of a contractural obligation, a duty of care, and of a need of others which it would be wrong for him to ignore. But they have this in common, that moral considerations either singly or resultantly so hedge him in as to exclude alternatives to a particular course of action. The analogy with legal necessity lies partly in the analogous role of principles and rules; and this use of 'must', like the closely related and more noticed use of 'ought', similarly serves to specify the content of moral demands rather than to invoke any practical necessity of conforming to them. The concept expressed I will refer to as that of moral necessity.

Collingwood's account appears to confuse practical necessity with compulsion. The concept of practical necessity is logically linked to that of compelling reasons for action, but not to that of acting under compulsion. But it is easy to replace or to treat as mere instances of practical necessity all Collingwood's references to compulsion. Kelsen is unexplicit, but in speaking of that 'absolute necessity' which can be founded only on a 'norm', he apparently refers to something of which legal necessity would be an instance. His theory deals in principles of a transcendent will from which morality, and strictly speaking even law, have not yet been distinguished. Practical, legal, and moral necessity thus seem to cover the ground which Collingwood and Kelsen are working on.

The three kinds of necessity have features in common. In each case it is only persons who must do something, or whose action can be said to be necessary. That to which the auxiliary verb 'must' or the adjective 'necessary' attaches can only be a term for something which can be done by some agent for whom it makes sense to frame the question of whether to do it. In other words, the question of what must be done or of what it is necessary to do in these senses can always arise from the point of view of an agent. Practical, legal, and moral necessity are in that sense all agent's concepts.

By contrast, causal and logical necessity both attach essentially to things which were, are, or will be the case. The verb 'must' and the adjective 'necessary' enter a wide variety of grammatical constructions. Where they do attach to a thing, or to something which that thing can do, there is no restriction to persons or even inanimate things, and the construction remains equivalent in force to a variety of others. Thus we can say that the *distance* between the billiard balls must be about to *increase*, or that some *change* in the position of the second ball must be about to *occur*. If we say as we strike a match that a flame must be about to appear, we do not refer to any physical object in which an effect is produced; and this in fact is an instance of causal necessity that has nothing to do with an effect, i.e., an instance of a cause without an effect. It may also be the struck billiard ball of which we say that it must be about to move. But in such a case, this statement about the ball and the effect produced in it is clearly equivalent to the statement that it *must be the case that* the ball will soon move, or that the motion of the ball is an event which must be *about to occur*.

It seems possible in favoured contexts to generate constructions of the actual family of 'A must do *x*', where A is nevertheless an inanimate object rather than a person, and the 'must' expresses causal or logical necessity; but in general the form resists this use of 'must'. We might, for example, say of a billiard ball that under conditions of a certain type it must move, since we can allow this 'must' the force of excluding cases of the ball not moving from the range of cases under discussion. But having arrived on an actual scene of collision, we are driven to saying that the ball must now *be about to* move, or be beginning to move, or be accelerating; to say that now *it must move* would indeed import a construction implying the existence of a point of view of the mover.

The difference in construction between saying in the present that A must be about to do x and that A must do x is made conspicuous by the reports of the same situations in the past tense. 'A must be about to do x' becomes 'A must have done x'. 'A must do x' certainly cannot take this form for the past; but only the unusual defectiveness of the English 'must' prevents us from using it at all (cf. Fr. 'Il a dû le faire'). We can sneak it into oblique contents, as in 'He found that he must do it'; otherwise we shift to 'It was necessary (for him) to do it' or 'He had to do it'. In the past tense, the 'must' of causal necessity as it were remains timeless, while the time of the event becomes past; the 'must' of practical necessity becomes past.

Analogous structural points apply to logical as well as causal necessity. 'Must', 'necessary', and 'necessarily' find their way into a wide variety of constructions in various tenses in uses which could be compared to those of a preceding 'so' or 'therefore'. The 'must' in 'The ball must be moving' or 'The ball must have moved' can be so used as to indicate that premises are available from which it follows that the ball is moving or that it moved. The variety of such constructions will nearly equal that of things which can follow, i.e., of propositions at least.

On the face of it the two groups of necessities are equally entitled to be called kinds of necessity, yet are utterly different in structure. What we need is a theory of necessity which gives an account of their common elements in such a way as to make intelligible both the contrast between the groups and the distinctions within them, including the distinction between logical and causal necessity. Hume's positive account of causal necessity has only to be taken seriously to provide the germ of such a theory. Appropriately developed, it locates the root of the positive analogy among all these necessities; from this root we can trace the growth of their differences. He said that the necessity was founded on the inference, rather than the inference on the necessity; the impression from which the idea of necessary connexion derives is an internal one, either of, or generated by, the transition of the mind to the idea of the effect. Let us say rather that the 'must' of causal necessity expresses the relation of the conclusion that the effect occurred, is occurring, or will occur to its empirical grounds when these grounds are empirically sufficient to exclude any alternative conclusion. For then we can say also that the 'must' of logical necessity expresses the relation of any propositional conclusion to some grounds which are logically sufficient to exclude any other conclusion. And the 'must' of practical necessity expresses the relation of a thing that can be done to the reasons for doing it where these reasons are sufficient to exclude any other course of action. Hume's own conceptions of logical derivability, of reasons, and of action utterly precluded his recognition of such a parallel, but need not inhibit us.

There is no difficulty in supposing that practical necessity is in some sense an aspect of the agent's deliberation. Hume was adventurous enough to suggest that causal necessity lay in an inference of the mind. It is no longer adventurous to hold that logical necessity does not govern the world, but in some sense governs our reasoning or even our way of speaking. Upon the whole, we may conclude, that necessity lies in the mind, and not in objects.

More literally, there is a link between the concept of necessity and the concepts of a reason, ground, or argument. But a reason for anything is always a reason for the doing of something which people in some wide sense *do*, whether for action or for saying something or thinking something or fearing something. In this sense reason is a faculty of the human mind. The analysis of practical necessity uses the concept of a reason for *action*; that of causal necessity, the concept of a ground for *thinking* that an effect has occurred, is occurring, or will occur; that of logical necessity, the concept of an argument for *saying* or *concluding* that something is so. This matching is part of the larger parallel between kinds of thinking. Kinds of question determine kinds of thinking about those questions, but in each kind we can identify the role of a consideration as tending either to settle the question or to give the thinker reason to settle it in some particular way. The successful outcome of his thinking is a recognition that the question is settled, or a settling of the question, which is in accordance with reason. The role of 'must' is to appear in the formulation of such an outcome, and there to indicate the appropriate type of conclusiveness of the reasons, grounds, or arguments which the thinker has.

This theory provokes in more general form the obvious objection to Hume's. His claim that the necessity lies in the inference is said to defy the presumption that it attaches to the effect. But this form both of the claim and of the objection is confused; let us restate the matter as follows. What we must account for, if we maintain that 'must' indicates an analogous relation in its various uses, is the structural contrast between the agent's concepts, on the one hand, and causal and logical necessity on the other. To the extent that the syntactical incidence of 'must' in such sentences as 'He must hang on to the boat' counts *for* the theory, surely the incidence of 'must' in such sentences as 'The ball must be about to move' counts *against* it.

Schematically there is a quite simple answer. If we consider forms of words representative of verbal expressions for the outcome of thinking, and then consider linguistic devices of general applicability which might add some expression of the conclusiveness of the reasons which support that outcome, we can then see, in outline at least, how the observed incidence of 'must' could come about, and why it might exhibit the observed asymmetry. Let us see how this works out.

Consider first forms of words which might serve as the expression in direct speech of the outcome of thinking. For the case in which the question of whether event E is about to happen has been settled, the obvious formulation is 'E is about to happen'. To find the cases relevant to 'He must hang on' we need to ask whose thinking is in question. According to the theory under examination, it is the agent's own thinking, i.e., the deliberation of the man in the water, or that of anyone who reflects on that deliberation from the point of view of the agent. So we ought to consider first forms of direct speech to express the agent's deliberation, and then forms of direct speech to express the spectator's reconstruction of deliberation for the same occasion.

It seems clear that to generate direct speech for the question of what to do we internalize the language of question and answer between the agent and another, assigning both roles to the agent. The agent can submit his deliberation to another by asking 'What shall I do?' The other can reply, according to his relations with the speaker, 'Do x' or 'You shall do x', or 'I should do x (if I were you)'. The other can ask for the outcome of deliberation with (the archaic) 'What shall you do?' or (the current) 'What will you do?' or 'What do you intend to do?' or the like; the simple answer is still 'I shall do x'. This can also serve as the agent's acceptance of the above three answers from the other. So we have 'Do x', 'You shall do x', and 'I shall do x', where the subject of the sentence, implicit or explicit, in each case refers to the agent, and similar forms with 'will'.[16]

Using these three forms, and 'E is about to happen', for outcomes of thinking, let us next consider the situation in which there is conclusive reason for doing x, or conclusive reason for saying that E is about to happen. That is the relevant occasion for asking how, to these verbal expressions of the outcome of thought, we might add an expression of the conclusiveness of the reasons which support it. In principle we might add an introductory conjunction, like 'so', or a change in emphasis, or some other linguistic device of general applicability. But suppose that in each case we make 'must' the modal part of the auxiliary to the main verb of the sentence. Then we produce the forms 'E must be about to happen' and 'I must do x', or 'You must do x'. In the theoretical case this adds a modal element to the auxiliary. In the practical case it probably replaces 'shall' or 'will' with 'must' throughout; but one might argue that it sometimes adds the modal element, depending on one's analysis of the grammatical structure of imperatives.

Finally let us include the third-person case. It does not matter whether we think of 'I must do x' and 'You must do x' as yielding directly the third-person 'He must do x', or whether we think of an underlying third-person deliberative question of the form 'What shall he do?' and its answer, 'He shall do x', to which the same modal substitution is applied. In either way we reach the desired form, 'He must do x'.

What these manœuvres show is that, if a fairly simple linguistic device, namely presence of 'must' in the modal position, carries the force of expressing the support of reasons for that outcome in whose expression it appears, then the present theory of necessity will pre-

16 Grammarians have not yet settled on a syntactic analysis of imperatives. See for example E. S. Klima, 'Negation in English', J. A. Fodor and J. J. Katz, eds., *The Structure of Language* (Englewood Cliffs : Prentice-Hall, 1964), pp. 258–60, and J. J. Katz and P. M. Postal, *An Integrated Theory of Linguistic Descriptions* (Cambridge, Mass. : M.I.T. Press, 1964), pp. 74–9, 149. It does not matter to the present issue what underlying modal is postulated to explain imperative forms; but the arguments for 'will' do not seem to me conclusive.

dict the distribution of 'must' which we actually find. In particular, we now see how it can come about that that distribution should mislead us. In the practical case, the 'must' becomes attached to an expression for a human action, and this action may actually coincide with that settling of the question of what to do for which there is conclusive reason. But in the theoretical case, the 'must' becomes inserted in an expression for an event, where this event may be of any kind, and this event will necessarily be distinct from that settling of the question of what happens for which there is conclusive reason.

On this reconstruction, the divergence comes about because of a peculiarity of questions of whether to do something. The action, embarking or deciding on which constitutes a settling of the question, is precisely what the question is about, and must be introduced into any formulation of the question. By contrast, the holding of a view, the thinking that something is so, or the saying that something is so, in which thinking can issue, has no place in the question considered in that thinking. The question of whether E is about to happen is about E, and not about my thinking or saying or in any sense doing anything, even when it is I who am doing the thinking about the question. Accordingly, in a formulation of my settling of the question, the inserted 'must' finds its way to grammatical association with E rather than with my mental operations. There seems no reason to regard this grammatical structure as abnormal or misleading. Hume's proper defence is to ask why anyone should base upon it a view that necessary connexion is other than it is. This theory of necessity thus offers an account of a concept of causal necessity taken as given, rather than a discrediting or unmasking of an alleged concept. Similarly Hume is at least open to interpretation as analysing the necessary connexion which actually holds among events, rather than as trying to show that there is no such thing.

3.4 THE SEARCH FOR THE BRUTE FACT

I now claim to have shown in outline how one can recognize a kind of necessity characteristic of causal relations, and give it an analysis which no more draws upon the concept of human action than does the analysis of logical necessity. I can accordingly claim the right to exploit concepts like causation and natural action as primitive with respect to my analysis of the point of view of the agent. It does not follow that there are no further elements which are uniquely found in the agent's thinking and which make the conceptual structure of deliberation irreducible to that of 'theoretical' inquiry. The experience of our own agency may be our special possession, even if we have more sense than to project it into nature.

I remarked at the beginning of this chapter that the empiricist programme for analysing the concept of human action was to look for the origin of the idea in our experience, and further, that this search typically addressed itself to one or another putative brute fact of personal experience. The leading candidates for this role of brute fact are the fact that we can produce effects in other things, the fact that we can move our bodies at will, and the fact that we can do anything at all at will. To confer on something the status of brute fact of personal experience is to herald the completion of the empiricist analysis, for it is to claim that the fact embodies primitive elements of the idea being analysed.

I will now begin my examination of this programme of analysis by an account of the relevant sense of bruteness in facts. This will enable us to see how each of the three facts referred to is a source of philosophical perplexity. This perplexity is in each case of a classical form, and seems inherent in the enterprise of analysis itself. Having formulated three questions to embody the corresponding perplexities, I will consider each in turn (in 3.5 to 3.7 respectively). It will then remain (in 3.8 and 3.9) to have a general reckoning with empiricism and to glimpse a further field of inquiry.

I take it that a fact is brute when, having stated it, we cannot do anything to explain it. If we cannot because at that point in our inquiry we lack an explanation which we need, then it is merely *as things stand*, or *for us now*, a brute fact. If we cannot because there is no explanation to be given, and it is out of place to call for one, then it can be assigned the status of being in the nature of the case a brute fact.

In either event, the explanation which cannot be given may be either an explanation of *why* it is a fact, or of *how* it is possible that it should be a fact. And the relevant necessity or possibility may be either empirical or logical.

Let us dismiss empirical perplexities, needing empirical explanations to resolve them, as not relevant to our present concern. For all that I can see, they are not even of much empirical interest in the case of the facts whose status we are considering. For example, with respect to the fact that I can move my body at will, we could ask for a scientific explanation of why I can, or could formulate empirical grounds for finding it remarkable that I can; but the relevant lines of biological and physiological inquiry seem obvious enough. Empirically speaking, the bruteness of the fact that I can move my body is pretty ephemeral.

What we need to remember is that we can ask for a logical explanation of how it is possible for an empirical fact to be a fact, as well as for a logical explanation of how it is possible for a logical fact to be a fact. Conceptual perplexity and wonder may have an empirical fact as their object.

Among conceptual perplexities, I think we can also dismiss quite quickly those which concern *why* the facts in question are facts. For example, philosophical perplexity about why it is that I can move my body in certain ways but not in others does not seem to me to have very deep roots. In surveying my body's repertory (2.8), we noticed the brute facts that I can raise my arm but cannot turn brown at will. The bruteness of these facts is just their logical contingency, and the lack of logical necessity in such facts, the absence of any conceptual reason why they are as they are, is worth remarking only because one might be tempted to look for such an explanation. And the temptation to do so was suggested largely by preoccupation with the intelligibility and unintelligibility of various questions of what to do, and by neglect of the point that a question can fail to make sense in particular circumstances for empirical reasons. I think the temptation has been satisfactorily disarmed.

The proper field of inquiry set for us by our apparent brute facts is conceptual rather than empirical, and the philosophical perplexity concerns not why these facts are facts but how it is possible that they should be facts. What we need is to understand why there should be any logical difficulties about these facts, and to see whether there is any way of meeting the difficulties.

Of course a general problem about how it is possible that I should be able to do things at will arises from determinism, and indeed from any view which recognizes the possibility of causal explanation of all the physical aspects of a single exercise of my ability. I cannot undertake to discuss difficulties coming from that source; in other words, I decline the problem of free will. But there remain perplexities which the point of view of the agent so to speak brings upon itself. We can formulate a question, in one of the classical forms of philosophical puzzlement, about each of the facts as follows: 1) How is it that I can produce effects beyond my body? More specifically, how is it that *I* can be said to do things which involve causal connexions extending indefinitely far beyond my body? 2) How is it that I can just move my body? 3) How is it that I am able to do anything at all at will?

These three questions of course are not the property of any given source of perplexity, and could be used to raise problems about free will. But I want to consider them as expressing difficulties which seem to be built into the enterprise of analysis. We become committed to the dilemma of either resolving any concept into its component elements or granting to that concept some kind of primitiveness. If it seems hard either to analyse a concept, or to see how it could be primitive, it will seem hard to understand how we can have such a concept at all. This is the sense in which the point of view of the agent brings these perplexities upon itself.

For a fact to have this kind of bruteness is for its concepts to resist analysis. If the concept of colour maintains in some analysis the position of a primitive element, then according to that analysis it is a brute fact that we see colours. That is why the search for the starting points of the analysis of human agency is at the same time the search for the brute fact of our agency.

We will find that the three questions are arranged in order of increasing difficulty. I will deal first with the fact that I can produce effects in other things (3.5). In 3.6 I will argue that the analysis of my ability to move my body at will does yield interesting and characteristic elements of our conception of our own action; but that there then remain elements which turn out to belong to any case of our action. Finally I will argue that the most stubborn of the three facts is the fact that I can do anything at all at will; the question of how this can be so is the most puzzling of the three. It is the question of how there can be such a thing as the point of view of an agent (3.7). But in the end I deny that any of these facts is finally, in the nature of the case, a brute fact.

3.5 HOW I PRODUCE EFFECTS

The first question, about how I can produce effects beyond my body, catches one source of strangeness in the form 'To do x is to do y'. For when doing x is bodily movement, and doing y is producing the effect which that bodily movement produces, the question 'How is it that to do x *is* to do y?' expresses the oddness of a thing which I clearly do, the bounds of which satisfactorily coincide with my own physical bounds, *turning out* to carry with it another thing which I do, the essence of which lies entirely beyond me, and the assignment of which to me depends on causal relations which happen to hold. And as Mr. Brian O'Shaughnessy remarks,[17] I do not do the causal connexions. That I discover them, and am thereby forced to admit that already, without doing anything further, I am producing an effect in another thing, is part of what is captured by the phrase '*is* to do y'.

If this were the whole difficulty, we could be reasonably assured that it was a problem in the combination of elements already available, and did not signal the entrance of some distinctive element of the agent's experience of action. This statement of the difficulty takes for granted the idea of bodily movement, and questions the attributability of effects produced by that movement to the mover or agent. It is an adequate response to show that in such a case my action parallels exactly that of an inanimate thing, and that the causal relation between mode of operation and effect produced provides as much basis for saying that I produce effects as for saying that a stone does. We have already looked at this parallel, and a much fuller account is given in Chapter 4.

But the question is also of more general application, since it covers the direct producing of effects, in which I have no mode of opera-

17 Brian O'Shaughnessy, 'The Limits of the Will', *Philosophical Review*, LXV (1956), p. 458.

tion. If I consider just myself and the effect produced, the direct relation between the two may seem nearer to the heart of the matter of human action. The disappearance from the concept of any causal relation between two events seems to force on our attention some peculiarity of human producing. And although the direct cases are oddities, they remind us that in the rest of the cases the attribution of an effect to me, which is implied in saying I produced it, by-passes the causal role of my body; I seem to claim the same relation to the effect regardless of whether I use means to produce it. Furthermore, when we reflect on the parallel with inanimate modes of operation, we see that the causal facts allow the effect to be attributed to *me* as a person only because the mode of operation is already a person's action. The movements of my body must be attributable to me as a person in order for their effects to be so attributable, just as a third link in any chain of effects will be attributable to me only if the second link is.

I think that it is indeed the case that the notion of my producing an effect has an aspect which differentiates it from that of an inanimate thing producing an effect. But, as we have seen, it is also the case that this difference is analogous to the difference between my moving when I move the parts of my body and my or a stone's moving when we fall. I do not think that the difference is exhibited to any advantage in the agent's experience of his own producing of effects. Indeed it is only when we study the spectator's point of view that it becomes possible to give a clear account of the difference. For, as I will argue in Chapter 4, and in 4.11 especially, a person's producing of an effect has to be analysed in terms of non-causal attributability of the effect to him, and so has a person's action in moving his body. But if we stick to looking at this non-causal attributability from the inside, i.e., from the point of view of the agent, there is nothing unique to the experience of action which distinguishes producing effects in other things from simply moving or from any other kind of action.

I conclude that the question of how I can produce an effect beyond my body is puzzling partly because it requires us to assimilate into our conception of action a variety of elements, including the apparatus of natural causation; partly because of the general notion of a physical event being attributable to me, which is equally exemplified in bodily movement; and partly for any reasons which attach to action in general. For the first I must rely on Chapters 2 and 4 to exhibit the connexion of elements; for the remaining two, on the next two sections.

3.6 HOW I KNOW THAT I AM RAISING MY ARM

The question of how it is that I can just move my body seems less easily dismantled. There seems more likelihood here of encountering irreducible concepts characteristic of the experience of human action.

In general, one expects to get light on the analysis of the concept of some kind of thing by asking how one knows various kinds of fact about things of that kind. I think it is particularly useful in the analysis of the agent's conception of his doing something to ask how he knows that he is doing it.

In the case of my moving my body, it is evident that my action entails the occurrence of motion in my body, where this motion is an ordinary empirical phenomenon. It seems to follow that I have ordinary empirical knowledge of when such a phenomenon does or does not occur. It has been traditional to note that I, like anyone else, can perceive the motions of my body, and to note that some conception of these motions capable of being exhibited in such perceptual experience will obviously be essential to my concept of my moving my body. Such a realization seems, for example, to be the defensible content of a curious doctrine of William James. He says

> When a particular movement . . . has left an image of itself in the memory, then the movement can be desired again, proposed as an end, and deliberately willed. But it is impossible to see how it could be willed before.[18]

Without accepting James' theory of willing, we can share his *a priori* assurance of a perceptual contribution to the concept of my moving my body.

On the other hand, occasion has often been found to doubt

18 William James, *The Principles of Psychology* (London: Macmillan, 1890), II, p. 487.

whether my knowledge of when my body does or does not move, even though such motion is always a physical event, is always ordinary empirical knowledge. In addition, the concept of my moving my body obviously includes and is more complex than the concept of my body moving, so that one might expect the analysis of how I know that I am moving my body to yield concepts not needed for the analysis of how I know that my body is moving. What actually emerges is an intermingling of two types of knowledge which is due to the simple if curious fact that I typically know that my body is moving *via* knowing that I am moving it; the analysis of the latter is accordingly needed even to complete the analysis of the former.

My knowledge of my body's motions seems peculiar in being knowledge of physical events which is in some sense direct or unmediated. One difficulty of identifying this directness is due to its being a compound of several kinds at once.

In the first place, my kinesthetic receptors give me a way of perceiving movement, position, pressure, and strain in my body which no one else happens to have. Others can look for themselves to see what I see; they are not wired up to feel what I feel. My doctor must therefore depend in practice on my reports of this way of perceiving my body. By contrast then with his knowledge of how my body feels, my own can be called direct, and this is an empirically necessary directness.

In the second place, a much subtler kind of directness in kinesthetic perception of my body has been pointed out by Mr. G. N. A. Vesey.[19] In showing the notion of 'knowledge without observation', used by Miss G. E. M. Anscombe in *Intention*, to be unclear, he was led to notice an unusual combination of characteristics in the way in which a person knows the position of his limbs. In his own terminology, this way of knowing differs from the way one knows that an insect is crawling up the back of one's neck in that it is not 'mediated perception'; there is nothing in one's present experience to explain how one perceives what one perceives. At the same time, it differs from the way one knows that something is red, in that the position of one's limbs is not a 'proper object' of kinesthesis as

19 G. N. A. Vesey, *The Embodied Mind* (London : Allen and Unwin, 1965), Chap. 7.

colour is of sight. These characteristics of feeling the position of one's limbs are shared by hearing the direction of a sound and by certain cases of seeing the distance of an object. His term for the kind of knowledge so gained is 'borrowed-meaning knowledge'.[20]

This analysis throws new light on perception of one's own body, and thereby, on perception of one's bodily action. Its interest lies partly in the fact that it accounts for some of the impression of a unique directness in one's way of knowing what one is doing, yet does so within a generally applicable analysis of perception.

But it seems far from a complete account of how one knows what one's body is doing, and it seems inadequate to account for the fact that, as Vesey himself says, 'the person knows that his hand has moved, when he moved it, solely by virtue of the fact that *he* moved it'.[21] Whatever our analysis of the agent's perception of his movements, we must face an old question: What is the difference between perceiving that one's arm is rising in the case in which one simply raises one's arm (or does so deliberately, by choice, etc.) and in the cases in which one does so involuntarily, or finds alarmingly that one seems to be doing it, or observes oneself doing it in a trance-like state? What is the difference even, in what one perceives, in the case in which one is disinclined to admit that one is doing anything, and one's arm simply rises? There may well be characteristic differences which are in a strict sense perceivable, both among these latter four cases and between all of them and that of simply raising one's arm. But it seems clear to me that even if there were no such differences, and the cases were perceptually indistinguishable, one would still just know which case it was. In particular, one would know whether one was raising one's arm in exercise of one's ability to do so at will, or whether this was not the case. I think, further, that this is so because in that case one knows that one is raising one's arm in a way which is independent of perceiving on that particular occasion the movement of one's arm. Such a way of knowing may be what Anscombe had in view, and it has still to be accounted for.

This way of knowing seems to combine irreconcilable features.

20 *Ibid.*, pp. 72, 106. Cf. the earlier version of Vesey's account, 'Knowledge without observation', *Philosophical Review*, LXXII (1963) pp. 204, 206, 209-10.
21 *Ibid.*, p. 106.

On the one hand, it is analogous to typical cases of introspection. Somewhat as I know that I am enjoying something, or am thinking about something, or seem at the moment to see something, so I know that I am raising my arm. If I cannot say whether or not I am enjoying it, or am thinking about it, or seem to see it, or am doing this, then it follows logically at least that it is not a standard case of any of these things. At the same time, the question of how I know seems out of place, and if pressed, to call for a mere reminder of the category of thing known, as in the technically phrased reply 'By introspection'. Again, my intention to do something in the future, the intention with which I am doing something, and the thing which I am intentionally doing, seem to be known to me in closely analogous ways. On the other hand, if one does call all these cases knowledge by introspection, the reach of introspection become surprising. If I can know in this way that I am raising my arm, *a fortiori* I can know in this way that my arm is rising. For the raising entails the rising. So it appears that I have introspective knowledge of the occurrence of a publicly observable physical event.

The way to avoid this contradiction is of course to admit that the knowledge is not simply introspective, and to admit that the question of how I know my arm is rising can have substantial content. We must recognize that a specific occasion can arise for asking how I know this, and that on such an occasion the answer can specify the modes of perception in play, as 'I can feel it' or 'I can see it rising'. This is conclusive against the suggestion that the knowledge is introspective. But what are the occasions for asking for perceptual credentials of the claim to be raising one's arm, and what are the implications of raising the question?

To point out that one can see one's arm rising is certainly relevant, because if one could see it not rising it would follow one was not raising it. But the occasion for doing so would normally be perceptually unusual, e.g., that one was a patient with an anesthetized arm, and was nevertheless raising one's arm. In ordinary circumstances the proprioceptors can be presumed to make visual perception unnecessary. It does not follow, from the fact that visual perception is relevant, either that it is essential to knowing that one's arm is rising or even that it is operative in the standard case.

To point out that one can feel one's arm rising is also relevant, since if one could feel it not rising it would follow that one was not raising it. In addition, kinesthetic perception does seem to be operative in the standard case. It seems to be an empirical fact about our nervous system that kinesthetic receptors are so placed and constituted as to keep constant track of our bodily movements. Consequently the occasion for pointing out their role need not be perceptually unusual. But there is nevertheless a sense in which kinesthetic perception, though operative in the standard case, has become inessential in the standard case. The actual appeal to it in defence of a claim to know that one is moving one's arm is more than a response to some imputation of doubt; it is a response to the implication that the case is non-standard in an executive rather than a perceptual way. In other words, the only occasion on which one needs to cite one's kinesthetic perception in defence of a claim to know is one on which there is question of a breakdown in one's power to move one's body at will.

Consider again the patient with anesthetized arm. It is customary to notice that the blindfold patient, when restrained, is surprised to find that he has not in fact raised his arm. What is more remarkable is the contrast between the presence and absence of restraint. When not restrained, the patient simply says that he is raising his arm, *and is right*. Here the absence of any kinesthetic sensation might be sufficient to occasion the question of how he knows he is raising his arm. If the answers 'I just know', or 'After all *I* am doing it', or 'By introspection' prove insufficient to warrant the claim to know, it will now be on the ground of the possibility that he is restrained, or paralyzed, or in some other way no longer in control of his body. If he discovers that he is wrong, for example by seeing that he is not doing what he thought he was doing, he thereby discovers that there is a breakdown in his power to do things.

In short, one does have ordinary perceptual knowledge that one's arm is rising. One does not have introspective knowledge that it is. But one does have a kind of conditionally introspective knowledge, in that one knows introspectively that one's arm is rising *provided all goes well*. All goes well when there is uninterrupted exercise of one's ordinary powers to do things at will.

I find a parallel here between Vesey's point that the position of a limb is not a proper object of kinesthesis and the fact that, so to speak, the motion of one's arm is not a proper object of introspection. The oddity of introspecting a motion bears some distant analogy to that of feeling a position or hearing a direction. Just as the latter oddity is somewhat diminished by reflecting on the process whereby kinesthetic or auditory experience gradually comes to play a role in perceiving position and direction, so the former is somewhat diminished by reflecting on the process whereby one acquires the ability to move one's body at will.

It is clear why my knowledge of the movements of my body is not ordinary empirical knowledge. It is unusual, first, because of the contribution of the proprioceptors. It is unusual, in the second place, though not unique, in the way to which Vesey has called attention; roughly, perception of position and motion of the body comes, through a process of learning, to depend on kinesthetic receptors, without there being any independently identified mediating kinesthetic experience. And finally, in acquiring my capacity to do things at will, which develops in the constant presence both of ordinary perception of my movements and of these unusual kinds of perception, I become able to tell that my body is moving, and to tell this in virtue simply of the facts that I am doing something, that I am doing it in exercise of my ability to do it at will, and that the thing which I am doing involves my body's moving in that way.

Let us take stock of the harvest, for an analysis of my concept of my raising my arm, of this much exploration of how I know that I am raising it. As long as we are dealing with perception rather than introspection, the kinds of directness of perception which have emerged seem to contribute to our present purposes only minor variations on the traditional theme already stated. If some motion in my body (*or* some effect on other things) is to provide me with a thing which I can consider doing, then that motion (or effect) must be perceivable by me somehow or other. Evidently at least part of my concept of that thing which I can do will be exhibited or given in my experience, namely in the perception alluded to, however exactly the perception works. Peculiarities in the perception are of interest here in showing how knowledge which is in various ways immediate or direct can nevertheless be perceptual. But it is the general classification of the knowledge as perceptual which is relevant to our present search for the elements of our analysis.

When we come, however, to the introspective aspect of my way of knowing, there are new issues.

3.7. THE EXPERIENCE OF DOING SOMETHING

We have reached a residue of the analysis of what it is for me, from my point of view as an agent, to move my body. It corresponds to the residue of the question of how I know that I am moving my body, i.e., to the introspective side of such knowing.

This introspective side of knowing that I am moving my body is not to be confused with a sensation or sensations of my body moving. A retreat from a full perceptual claim about my body will lead to a report of sensations, e.g., that it looks and feels to me now just as if my arm were rising. This could be called locating the sense-data of bodily movement, and the sensations themselves are events known by introspection. If I begin from the claim that I am now of my own free will raising my arm, or that I am now involuntarily raising my arm, the same progressive withdrawal of perceptual claims will lead to the report that it looks and feels to me now as if I were raising my arm (of my own free will or involuntarily, as the case may be). The sense-data of these two kinds of action may or may not be characteristically different from the sense-data of the body moving on its own. But it is unimportant whether they are or not. To rephrase the assertion made in the last section, even if the sense-data are indistinguishable, I will still just know whether I am simply raising my arm, or whether, on the other hand, I am raising it involuntarily or it is rising by itself. And if I do just know that I am simply raising it, this conditional introspective knowledge is distinct from my knowledge that I have the sense-data of bodily movement. The route to isolation of the introspection of action does not lie through the progressive reduction of perceptual claims.

This distinction between sensation and the introspectible aspect of action is made clearer by another consideration. Introspectively knowing that I am moving my body is not different in principle from introspectively knowing that I am producing an effect in something else. As I can also perceive the movements of my body, so I can also perceive the effects produced. As I just know that I am raising my arm, provided all goes well in my body, so I just know that I am turning left at the crossroads, provided all goes well in my body and in my car, and that I am writing a word on the blackboard, providing all goes well in body, chalk, and board. The difference between the two types of case lies in differences between proprioceptors and other receptors, between bodily skill and manipulative skill, and so on. What is in common among them all is knowing that I am doing something. We can ignore the sensory content of my experience of moving my body; and we can ignore the distinction between moving my body and producing effects in other things. The tendency to feel that 'voluntary control of the body' contains the heart of the concept of action may perhaps be justified by the use we have already made of this distinction, and by the perceptual peculiarities we have already noticed. But it is an illusion to suppose that that residual concept which we are seeking in the introspection of action has anything in particular to do with the body. We can set aside both the question of how I can produce effects in other things and the question of how I can move my body in favour of the third question. Whatever the particular kind of thing I might do, how is it that I can do it at will?

It seems to be a brute fact that I can do things at will. For it seems that my concept of thus doing something either is or has at its centre a concept that must be taken as primitive; the bruteness of the fact is our inability to analyse this concept.

The empiricist interpretation of this impasse is that the nature of this kind of action is something the agent must simply experience. The best we can do by way of introducing such a concept into the analysis is to direct attention to the occasions on which it is exemplified, and rely on each person's experience of those occasions. As for colours or for pain, we must rely on ostensive definition or on something analogous to it. But the relevant experience will have to be introspective.

Locke provides classic expression of such a view when he makes power a simple idea of reflection.

> Power *also is another of those simple* ideas *which we receive from* sensation *and* reflection. *For, observing in ourselves that we can at pleasure move several parts of our bodies which were at rest; the effects, also, that natural bodies are able to produce in one another*

occurring every moment to our senses, we both these ways get the idea of power.[22]

Then in the chapter on power he has a more developed account which leans toward the identification of active power with the will.

> *But yet, if we will consider it attentively, bodies, by our senses, do not afford us so clear and distinct an* idea of active power, *as we have from reflection on the operations of our minds....*

> *The* idea *of the beginning of motion we have only from reflection on what passes in ourselves, where we find by experience that barely by willing it, barely by a thought of the mind, we can move the parts of our bodies which were before at rest....*[23]

This Cartesian passage might suggest that the empiricist interpretation is committed to a dualistic analysis of doing something at will, in terms of an act of volition which precedes or accompanies the physical phenomena. I see no such commitment. Let us insist as firmly as we please that in raising my arm the only act which is in question is the act of raising my arm. We can still be impressed by an apparent impossibility of analysing the concept of such an act without reference to the sheer experience of what it is like to do the thing. It is this latter view, that the analysis can only be completed by this experience, which I am now considering.

There are two difficulties with the view. First, the desired element of the analysis is, on the face of it, complex, whereas the point of asserting dependence on an experience is the implication that this element is unanalysable. That which is supposed to be characteristic in the experience is precisely that the action in question is an exercise of one's power to do things at will, and that one is doing a thing which one *can* either do or not do, at will. How can Locke suppose that a *power* is a simple idea, or that the perception of a power in a physical object or the introspection of a power in the mind is like seeing a colour? The logical structure of the concept expressed by 'can' is usually complex and elusive. Why in this case should the word express a concept given by a simple experience?

22 Locke, *An Essay Concerning Human Understanding*, ed. J. W. Yolton (London : Dent, 1961), Book II, Chap. VI, Sec 8.

23 *Ibid.*, Book II, Chap. XXI, Sec 4.

Similar embarrassment follows libertarian attempts to oppose an articulate determinism with the savouring of an introspection.[24]

The second objection is more decisive. In order to have the experience, the agent must actually do something, and he must do it in exercise of his capacity to do it or not at will. But in order to do something in this way, he must already have the concept of doing something in this way. So there cannot be some element of the concept which waits to be given by the experience.

The reasons why he must already have the concept also reveal why it is that the instances of the concept are known by introspection to be occurring. For to say of the agent without qualification that he is doing something (or in particular cases to say that he is doing it of his own free will, or because he chooses to, or voluntarily, etc.), is in part to say of him a) that the question of whether or not to do it arises for him, and b) that his doing of it is, or is the outcome of, the settling of the question. (A fuller exposition of this view is given in 4.5). But these two conditions together imply that he is aware that the question of whether to do the thing arises, that he is aware of what he is doing, and that he is aware that he could have not done it. In the absence of awareness of any one of these things, his actions will not count as an exercise of his ability to do things at will. Awareness of these things in turn requires possession of the concept of the question of whether to do something, and the concept of ability not to do it. And possession of these concepts implies possession of the concept of being able to do something at will. But the same necessity of being aware that the question arises, and that he could have not done it, implies the necessity of being

24 Professor Richard Taylor, in his book *Action and Purpose* (Englewood Cliffs : Prentice Hall, 1966), p. 5, says that 'I can move my finger' means in part that whether or not I do it is 'within my power', and remarks : 'And this is certainly a philosophically baffling expression which I feel sure no one can ever analyze'. Although Taylor's book treats many of the topics of this book, I had completed my own account, and it did not seem practicable to start plotting its relations to his. But on the issue of the unanalysability of this use of 'can' and of the concept of an act (*ibid.*, pp. 91 ff.), let me make one remark. I have given some reasons for denying that such concepts cannot be analysed, and I have not been convinced by Taylor's reasons for saying they cannot be, but I doubt that the issue of possibility is fruitful; it will be up to me to produce actual analyses, and to Taylor to refute them.

aware that he is doing the thing in exercise of his ability to do it or not at will. And when we say of him that, on any occasion on which he exercises his ability to do a thing or not at will, he must be aware that he is doing so, this is just what we mean by saying that this is known to him by introspection. As to the difference between this kind of action and others, it is not a case of the agent knowing the difference just by experiencing it; it is a case of his experience of just knowing the difference.

The appearance of circularity in this account must be faced rather than evaded. The concept of an event or state which involves awareness of that same state appears to involve a vicious regress. My partial analysis of the ability to do something at will perhaps makes it easier to understand how there can be a kind of *action* such that the agent's possession of the concept of that kind of action, and his awareness of each instance of the concept, are essential to the occurrence of an instance—in other words, how there can be a kind of action which is essentially self-conscious. But my analysis does very little to resolve the perplexity which is generated by the notion of self-consciousness in application to any psychological event or state, whether action or belief or passing thought. That no vicious regress is incurred would have to be shown by an adequate analysis of awareness, in short by an adequate account of introspection.

I cannot undertake such an account here. What I claim for present purposes is that the accessibility to introspection of doing things or not at will is grounded in that same structure of the concept which guarantees that the agent will possess the concept independently of his having the experience of such action. We are thereby precluded from regarding the experience as the indispensable source of a concept not further analysable. This empiricist view came on the scene as an interpretation of the apparent bruteness of the fact that I can do things at will. For we did seem to have tracked down an elusive but irreducible element of the agent's concept of his action. The present account not only rejects the supposed data of inner sense offered in place of analysis; it begins to exhibit part of the analysis. It therefore provides some evidence itself that the impossibility of further analysis, and the bruteness of the fact, are merely apparent.

Why then the appearance? How can we account for the impression that the analysis had reached a limit, and that this was the limit at which experience had to take over? I think the analysis had reached one sort of limit, and that a legitimately identifiable experience happened to be on hand; but the limit was not one to which the experience was relevant. For the limit reached was set merely by the point of view from which this investigation has been conducted. We have not merely selected for attention that kind of doing for which there is a point of view of the agent, we have largely confined the discussion itself to that point of view. The questions of what I can do to other things, how I can or cannot move, how I know what I am doing, and so on, were all raised from the agent's point of view. On completing our partial review of the range of questions of what to do which can arise for me as an agent, we were left with the general phenomenon of such questions being open to the agent to settle. The fact that the agent can do something *at will* is the fact that the question of whether or not to do it is open to the agent. We were left then with the general question of how there could be any question of what to do. But this is just the question of how there can be such a thing as the point of view of the agent. The question can be investigated as far as one pleases, but not from the point of view of the agent. The sense of impasse arises from not realizing that, in order to understand fully a point of view from which we have been considering certain problems, we must leave that point of view. The impossibility of resolving our perplexity from that point of view is mistaken for an absolute impossibility. As long as we rest where we are, there is nothing to do but savour the experience of being there.

3.8 EMPIRICISM AND THE OPERATIONS OF THE MIND

In sections 3.2 and 3.3 of this chapter I followed Hume in pursuit of the origin of the idea of inanimate action. Having reached that necessity with which the effect occurs, I agreed with him in tracing it to an inference of the mind, and accepted this as his major insight; but I also offered an account which he could not accept of the relations between necessity and human reasoning. In the next four sections of the chapter (3.4 to 3.7) I considered, from the point of view of the agent, how it is that I am able to do various things, and how I know what I am doing, in order to locate any peculiarities of the agent's concept of human action. Having reached the sheer experience of doing something which I just know that I can do or not at will, I have admitted that the analysis can go no further without leaving the point of view of the agent and subjecting that point of view itself to analysis; but I have denied that this experience is the indispensable source of unanalysable elements of the concept of human action. In both enterprises I have had to follow traditional empiricist analyses for a good distance. But I have declined to accept either Hume's secondary impression derived from the inference of the mind, or Locke's simple idea of power gained from reflection, as an end-point for the analysis. In the first section of the chapter I promised to show how the form of the empiricist programme vitiated its results at the last stage of each analysis, and this I now try to do.

When Hume wants to analyse a concept, he asks for the impressions from which the idea is derived. In order to show the limitations imposed by this approach, let us state it as a special case of a more general inquiry. The empiricist tradition has tried to throw light on the nature of things known, by turning to the nature of knowledge and of the mind which does the knowing. But in doing so it has always fallen short of full and unprejudiced attention to the operations of the mind in general. Suppose that we state such an enterprise in terms like the following. For any concept whose analysis is in question, let us consider the operations of the mind in which that concept has a role, and ask what other operations of the mind logically must be involved in these. For example, let the understanding of an effect be the operation of the mind in which the concept of cause has a role; and let my producing of an effect in something be the operation of the mind in which the concept of 'power' has a role. If we now ask from what *impressions* the ideas of cause and of power derive, we are engaged in part of this general inquiry. We are asking for operations of the mind which fall in the category of *the having of impressions* and which are logically involved in the operations of understanding an effect or producing an effect. (The having of impressions I take to be a category including sensation and introspection.) But from the point of view of this same general inquiry, the effect of Hume's question is restrictive; it encourages us to insist that all operations of the mind be eventually analysed in terms of sensation and introspection.

On a liberal interpretation of Hume's question, it may indeed restrict only the form and not the content of the analysis. For the having of impressions includes introspection, and introspection is a channel through which we can introduce any operation of the mind which is relevant; in that case the distortion affects only the way of stating the analysis. As the empiricist cannot introduce constant conjunction except by the sensory experience of constant conjunction, so he cannot introduce an inference except by the introspection of the inference. But there is no restriction on the nature or complexity of introspected operations of the mind. For example, even though we conceive of introspection as passive, on the model of perception, we can conceive of it having an activity as its object, on the model of the perception of physical motion and change. If that which is introspected can be either an undergoing or a doing, even a doctrine of introspection as inner sense need create no bias for the passive as against the active.

In principle this is an adequate defence of Hume's narrower question, at least against the charge of logically excluding a range of possible analyses. But let us observe, in the two cases in hand, whether the effect of this programme has not turned out in practice to be fatally restrictive. Perhaps the restrictive effect has been aggravated by a temptation to suppose, at the point at which introspection has to be invoked, that it provides a *simple* impression, and thereby to bring the analysis to a halt before the introspected operation of the mind can yield its full contribution.

Thus Hume's impression from which the idea of necessary connexion is derived arises from an inference of the mind. But if this were really just the introspective entrance into the analysis of the concept of the inference itself, we would expect much more to be done with this concept. Evidently the theory of inductive inference, including the conditions under which we can say that the effect *must* occur, would then be actually a part of the analysis of causation. But Hume's account comes to rest, and his insight bears no further fruit, because this mysterious impression, whose name or content is never given, is treated like a funny feeling. As a simple sensation, or the introspective analogue of one, it can only be savoured. From the point of view of the generalized analysis of the operations of the mind, the introspection of the inference has usurped the place of the inference itself as an element of the analysis of causal explanation.

Again, in pursuit of the brute fact of my agency, we were led, as Locke was, past a variety of sensations involved in my perception of my action to a residue of the concept which was not reducible to sensations. Since this residue corresponds to the introspection of my action, the empiricist is again tempted to invoke the unanalysable experience of doing something, even at the cost of inventing a simple quasi-sensation of introspection. From an unrestricted point of view, the alternative is straightforward. The operation of the mind which is needed as element of the analysis is not the introspection of the action, but the action itself. A predilection for brute facts, given in experience, diverts the analysis from the element sought, which is not the brute fact that I can raise my arm, but the brute raising of my arm. Nor is this an unanalysable operation of the mind; it is merely the one we treat as primitive so long as we elect to maintain the point of view of the agent. At the same time we can suspect that the empiricist preference for an experience or quasi-sensation, over the action itself, is associated with a bias in favour of empirical (and in general, theoretical) concepts, and a reluctance to admit irreducibly practical concepts into the analysis. My own insistence on the point of view of the agent is a protracted struggle against this tendency.

3.9 THE CATEGORY OF OPERATIONS OF THE MIND

The phrase 'operations of the mind' is an undefined piece of jargon which so far has served a merely schematic purpose. To replace it successfully with a precise set of related categories or sub-categories would be the fruit of a long inquiry. For now, I merely notice some of the categories in which this one might be included or which could be distinguished within it.

Clearly we are dealing with things which people can in the widest sense be said to do. But this category, encompassing everything for

which there is an active verb taking a personal subject, is too wide
to be useful. Within it we want to confine ourselves somehow or
other to things which in some way involve the person's mind, or
manifest the qualities or states of his mind.

One category that no doubt falls within the desired one is that of
things which people do which are at least sometimes conscious
i.e., which people know themselves introspectively to be doing in
at least some of the cases in which they do them. This category is
cut across by distinctions of passivity and activity, and includes
instances from all along the spectrum. Visual sensation seems a
paradigm of the passive end, and invites formulations with 'have' as
well as 'do'; voluntary physical action seems a paradigm for the
active end; between are pain, believing, remembering, inferring,
fearing, wanting, wondering, and deciding. This category is also cut
across by certain divisions into mental and physical, such as the one
noticed in 2.1; only dualistic prejudice stands in the way of counting physical action as an operation of the mind.

Within this category of things which people do which are sometimes conscious, there is a narrower one which will prove of special
interest. It is the category of things which people do of which it can
be said that there are reasons for doing them (and that people have
reasons for doing them). At this step the narrowing is such as to
exclude sensation. It does not make sense to speak of my reasons
for having a visual sensation or for feeling pain, though there will
of course be causal reasons why I have sensations. This is one of the
features in virtue of which sensations are said to be *given*. The sub-
category which has so far been our subject, that of things about
which it makes sense to frame the question of whether to do them,
clearly belongs among the things which people can have reasons for
doing. But it is far from exhausting them. The traditionally obvious
cases have been intellectual operations of the mind like concluding
or believing. (The quantity of recent writing on practical reason has
by now made it almost easier to understand how there can be
reasons for action than to understand how there can be reasons for
belief.) But there can also be reasons for liking, wanting, and fearing.

The category just identified constitutes by definition the range of
reasons for anyone's doing anything, in the widest sense of 'do', and
consequently constitutes in one sense the scope of the faculty of

reason. Eventually one would like to define purely psychological categories of the same extension. That might help to explain why there can be reasons for some of the things people do but not for others, and might help to explain how reasons for action resemble and differ from reasons for believing and for wanting. Such an account would explain the scope of reason and explain the versatility of reason. In the meantime the present demarcation of this category will be useful in reminding us that some features of reasons for action belong to reasons in general, while some are peculiar to the field of action. It is also useful through providing the range of the theory of modal concepts adumbrated (for the case of necessity) in 3.3. I conjecture that modal concepts in general express the pressure of reason for or against doing things which people do. If so, the theory of modal concepts and the theory of the faculty of reason will run parallel, and the scope of both will be given by that category of operations of the mind which consists of the things which people can have reasons for doing.

4 The attribution of effects

In Chapter 2 I used the distinction between inanimate and human action in terms of which to describe, from the point of view of the agent, the role of the agent's body in providing the basic content of his action. This distinction itself presented a problem, that of relating the contrasting differentiæ of these two species of doing, and this problem remains unsolved. But the distinction also served to introduce two more problems. I went on in Chapter 3 to examine, for each kind of action, a traditional enterprise of analysis. With regard to inanimate action, as a species of causation in nature, I considered the problem of accounting for that necessary connexion which seems needed, along with constant conjunction, to complete the analysis of causation. I rejected the idea that any element of the analysis was an anthropomorphic projection of human action, and to this extent defended the exploitation of the concept of natural action in the analysis of human action. With regard to human action, I considered the problem of locating the brute fact of our own agency and the prospect of thereby identifying elements peculiar to the analysis of human action and given only in introspective experience. I declined to admit the irreducibility of the concept of human action except under the self-imposed limitation of the point of view of the agent. In the light of these investigations, what status can be assigned to each of the two kinds of action, and what rationale can be given for the very distinction between inanimate and human action?

So far inanimate action, as a species of causation in nature, has kept roughly the status assigned to it by Hume, except for some re-interpretation of his account of necessity. The main elements of the analysis are thus, first, constant conjunction or some version of this concept, in terms say of necessary and sufficient conditions or law-like hypotheticals; and second, necessity of a kind analysable in terms of reasoning in accordance with such hypotheticals. I have also suggested (cf. 2.2 and 2.3) that the differentia of natural action within natural causation can be provided in terms of the attributing of effects to events which consist in physical things doing things. This is the merest sketch, in the case both of causation and of natural action, and it will be one of the tasks of this chapter to fill out both the genetic and the differential accounts (4.9 and 4.10).

As to human action, the structure of the account has marked off that kind of human doing for which there exists a point of view of the agent, and under this heading the main cases of action selected for study have been those in which the human agent fills pretty exactly the role of an inanimate agent in the production of effects and in motion or change. I am inclined to set down, as the most striking thing about the account so far, the extent to which thinking that is carried on *from* the point of view of the agent is carried on *in* concepts which are accessible equally to the spectator, because they belong to that neutral field for which the distinction between agent and spectator is not drawn. Natural action and the agent's body, as ordinarily perceived, have supplied most of the analysis, and the effort to track down some distinctive and irreducible ele-ment ended only in a reminder that it was, after all, the point of view of the agent that the analysis had itself taken up. Very little has been done to make clear the way in which my use of the point of view of the agent implicitly selects a kind of action. In particu-lar we need an explicit account of the differentia of this kind of action as a species of human doing. It is a second task of this chap-ter to supply this account (4.5 and 4.6).

It remains to explain the similarities and differences between in-animate and human action, and to give some rationale for the con-trasting differentiæ of the two kinds. This is a third task for this chapter, and it is the most inclusive and complex of the three. It becomes the occasion for offering a rudimentary theory of what action is (esp. 4.12).

It turns out that for all three tasks we need to examine action from the point of view of a spectator. Of course, anything which can be said neutrally can be assigned vacuously to the point of view of the spectator as well as to that of the agent, so that there is no occasion to restrict ourselves to those cases for which the distinction is drawn. The very question which will engage us is what it is for the spectator, observing an effect in nature, to attribute that effect to inanimate agency or to agency for which there exists a point of view of the agent. It turns out further that this concept of attributability is the key to an understanding both of causation in nature and of the differing differentiæ of inanimate action and human action.

The order of the exposition will be as follows. Sections 4.2 to 4.6 review the types of action to be covered by the analysis, restate the differentiæ of inanimate and human action, and consider the problem of constructing out of the features of the cases considered a theory which covers all the types and explains the differentiæ. It is in the course of this survey, in 4.5 and 4.6, that I undertake my second task of expounding the differentia of human action. Then in sections 4.7 to 4.12 I develop an analysis in terms of explanatory attributability. The early part of it embodies, in 4.9 and 4.10, my attempt on the first task of showing how inanimate action is a species of natural causation. The later part proceeds from causal attributability to non-causal attributability, and uses this pair of ideas in the resulting theory of action. Finally, the last section of the chapter examines some implications.

4.2 BODY AND SOUL

The discussion will juxtapose human action and inanimate action without reference to the levels of animate behaviour in between. Eventually we need an explanation of why animal behaviour does not count as action at all except in rare and marginal cases. I suspect that animal behaviour is one of those fields which not only is troublesome to the analyst of the natural language but also puts some strain on the resources of the natural language itself. Human action and inanimate action are, in our experience, and in practice, inextricably intermingled; it may turn out that a concept well adapted to function in this area of intermingling is not well adapted to deal with intermediate cases. It strikes me that our conception of animals undergoes simultaneous temptations to anthropomorphism and to mechanism. But however that may prove, it is prudent in the meantime to leave animals (and also artifacts) out of account, and to offer as one's first approximation a theory applicable just to persons and inanimate things.

It will nevertheless be helpful to begin by recalling certain points which hold for other living things as well as persons.

It is the peculiarity of animate things to have a soul. It is therefore also their peculiarity to have a body. For a stone, a planet, an apple, and a severed head do not (in the required sense) have a body; they are bodies. Hence the neat exclusiveness of Strawson's phrase 'things which are or possess material bodies'.[1] The phrase is less adequately inclusive. Even if one can include seas and mountains under 'bodies of water' and 'bodies of rock or earth', there are many physical things, including many inanimate agents, which lack the discreteness or permanence or solidity to qualify as bodies (e.g., river beds, clouds, waves, and reflections). Nevertheless, among agents, bodies are the paradigms of easily identifiable and re-identifiable agents, and from the point of view of the spectator of animate action the contrast between things which have and are bodies is a natural and operative one. Living organisms (I am using 'soul' in the Aristotelian sense in which 'animate' means both 'living' and 'having a soul') do as a matter of empirical fact generally have, as well as internal complexity, the discreteness, permanence, and solidity of typical material bodies; and when they die they are just bodies. In other words, the body which a living thing has *is* a body; but the living thing itself is not. Since it makes a difference whether a given effect is attributable to a living thing, or to its body, or to both, the contrast between having and being a body is constantly in play.

Having a body suggests not having a body. If having *a* body (at all) is like having two hands or having a house, one might with more or less inconvenience have got along without any of them. Talk of embodiment, without protestations of necessity, suggests a process of

1 P. F. Strawson, *Individuals* (London : Methuen, 1959), pp. 39, 46.

which disembodiment would be the reverse—a traffic between our actual and an alternative condition. But a person has a body only as he has the five senses, and has a mind, and has a past. To say any of these things is just to say that there exists a certain type of fact *about the person*. My abilities in colour discrimination are facts about my senses; my slowness is a fact about my mind; my weight is a fact about my body; all are facts about me. It is *I* who have physical properties and participate in causal interactions even though I and my body are not identical. In particular a person has *a* body as inevitably as he has a past; I will not escape my spatial properties by going elsewhere, any more than I will get rid of my past however long I work on the problem.

So a person, as an animate agent, is not a body, but merely has one; and yet his physical properties are his, and not merely his body's. The subtlety of this relation puts a strain on the concept of a part. Head, feet, and back are obviously parts of me; this is especially clear when the creature concerned is passive (e.g., 'My ears were the coldest parts of me', 'He was burned on all his exposed parts', 'She stepped on some part of the cat'). However, there is also a temptation to say that my hand is part of my body rather than part of me. This is especially strong when I am active, and also when my body is, for there is then occasion to distinguish the two kinds of activity. When I move my hand, or push something away with my hand, this entails that my hand moves, or that my hand pushes the thing away; but the entailment does not hold the other way. When my hand moves, or pushes something, it may be the case that I do not do anything at all; but it is entailed that my body moves, and that my body pushes something. That my hand moving should entail my body moving but not me moving strongly suggests that my hand is part of my body but not part of me. The suggestion is fallacious, but its plausibility is instructive.

These entailments and failures of entailment are the stock-in-trade of analyses of action. The question is often asked what there is to my moving my hand in addition to my hand moving. Looking at this question from the point of view of the agent, i.e., from the point of view precisely of a person for whom there arises a question like that of whether to move his hand, we found that the desired difference or complement was strangely elusive. I concluded that it was elusive because it was built into the very point of view from which we were looking for it. We will see what light can be cast on it by looking at it from the point of view of the spectator. To him, one notices, my hand moving and my moving my hand are superficially much alike. He is not committed, in any given case, to supposing that there is such a thing as the point of view of the agent.

4.3 FIVE CASES OF ACTION

In Chapter 2 I picked out some cases of action and arranged them in one of the orders which might seem illuminating to an embodied soul. As an agent he was necessarily also an observer of nature, and was confronted by the phenomena of inanimate action and of inanimate motion and change; he could well see his own action as a participation in these phenomena, and one which he owed to his body. This chapter has now to survey the same cases in the same order, as they seem to another agent who remains an observer of nature. As a spectator of the interaction of bodies, he will see the participation of the human agent as the appearance on the scene of an animate body. The relevant range of phenomena can be represented by five cases, one of inanimate action and four of human action.

I will be arguing later that, in order to see why doing is action in these cases but not in some others, we must take into account the explanatory force of reports of action. So it will be convenient to accompany the description of the five cases with comment on the ways in which the spectator not merely recognizes but also understands the things he sees happen.

Any of our usual examples would do for inanimate action. Let us suppose for our first case that 1) a log (itself perhaps floating and carried forward by the waves) pushes some sand along on a beach. By the analysis already given, the action of the log on the sand consists in its producing an effect in the sand, namely motion, by pushing on it. It is sufficiently obvious that the report of what the log does includes a causal explanation of the motion of the sand.

The substitutability of human action might be underlined by considering a person who does the same thing, but to keep the cases distinct let us revert to the breaking of the branch of a tree, as done by wind, falling tree, or person. Suppose next that 2) a person, in the course perhaps of clearing a path, breaks a branch with his hand. This report of what happens has the same structure as a report of inanimate action, for we can identify the agent, the agent's mode of operation, and the effect produced in something else, and the report includes a causal explanation of this effect; it is just that the agent is a person. The spectator could normally see straight off that what happened was that a person pressed down on the branch with his hand until he broke the branch; this counts by ordinary standards as a report of a directly observable event. At the same time the effect on the branch is implied to be attributable to what the person did, to the pressure he put on the branch, to his action, to his agency, to him. The event is a case of that kind of human action for which there exists a point of view of the agent.

A second account of the same event is simultaneously available to the spectator. It is less usually expected or offered, it is less complete, but it is correct and compatible with the first account. The spectator could see that the person's hand pressed down on the branch until it broke it. This report too has the same structure, with the hand as agent; the effect is attributable to the pressure of the hand, to the action of the hand, to the agency of the hand, to the hand. The explanatory force of this report rests on just the sort of physics which serves for case 1) and for the falling of trees; the hand's breaking of the branch is in a sense a case of inanmate action imbedded within case 2).

Let case 3) be one in which a person breaks the branch of a tree by hitting it with an axe. This case can be regarded as case 2) with a whole chain of inanimate action imbedded in it. The hand moves the axe, the axe breaks the branch.

Next consider the empirically rare phenomenon of a person's direct producing of effects. To use the example from 2.7 of a person blowing on something, suppose that 4) a person blows sharply out. He makes the air stream out of him, but without doing anything else by which he makes it move. Here again the spectator can, at least on the basis of more sophisticated observation, give both of two different explanations of the effect on the air. One of them attributes it to the action of the person's lungs, the other to the action of the person. But the second kind of action lacks a mode of operation; as to how the person blew the air out, we can only say that he just blew it out, as he is able to do, and not by doing anything else at all. For he did not contract his lungs, and may not know that he has lungs; when he breathed, his lungs contracted.

Although the person does not contract his lungs, it is evident that their contraction is in some sense an aspect of what he does. Towards specifying the sense in which it is an aspect, we can say first that the contraction does provide the actual explanation of the effect on the air, which effect is attributed to the person by the report of what he does. And further, this fact helps to support an explanation of the contraction itself; evidently the lungs contracted because the person was breathing out. This explanation does not proceed by assigning a cause to the contraction, but depends on an account of what actually happens when a person breathes. The inanimate action of a part of the body is again imbedded in the human action, but in a different way from that of the hand in cases 2) and 3).

Finally, let us suppose that 5) a person nods his head. This is a case of his merely moving, as when he steps forward or holds out his hand. It is clearly action, and as with the preceding cases of human action, that kind of action for which there exists a point of view of the agent. Evidently, since cases 2) and 3) involve the person using his hand to press on the branch and to lift the axe respectively, action of the type of 5) is embedded in these other cases. They are standard cases of manipulation, and they depend on sheer bodily movement for their basic modes of operation. But in case 4) the blowing does not so depend and no action of the type of 5) is implied.

Superficially there is a close similarity between the report of an inanimate thing moving and the report of a person moving. One cannot report action and the other can, but there appears no ground for this difference in the form of the report or in the relation between the motion reported and the effects it produces. Both reports appear to be descriptive in force rather than explanatory. It is not merely that, whether A is a thing or a person, the report of A doing x does not explain why A does x, which is only to be expected; but also it is not at first obvious that the report explains anything else, as the report that the log moved the sand does explain the motion of the sand. That the log merely moved; that the person merely moved; these seem pure phenomena. However, as I will argue in 4.11, we may ask, with respect to the motion of the head in case 5), what else is entailed by the full report that the person nodded his head, and whether it contributes anything to the understanding of why the head moved. It seems that it must contribute something, since it is informative to say that the person's head nodded *because* he nodded it. The theory of action to be sketched will contain some account of what information is conveyed.

We have then the following five cases of action. 1) A log pushes some sand along a beach. 2) A person breaks a branch with his hand. 3) A person breaks a branch by hitting it with an axe. 4) A person blows sharply out. 5) A person nods his head.

4.4 THE DIFFERENTIA OF ACTION

A's action will be A's doing something. Any kind of action will be some kind of doing on the part of an agent. This much is truistic, but suggests that we could ask for an account of action *per genus et differentiam*. Given a specification of the kind of thing that can be an agent, what kind of doing by such a thing counts as action?

Those who conclude that 'action' has more than one sense can ask the corresponding question about each sense distinguished. But the onus of proof lies in general on those who wish to draw distinctions of sense, and when they succeed they generally have a residual problem, whatever its nature is, of explaining how there come to be just the senses distinguished. Further, I find that I am unclear as to when the facts show two senses and when they show two species of thing under one sense of the word. I think it is possible to postpone this issue by speaking of different kinds of action, since this phrase appears to be neutral between the two alternatives. I have adopted this course so far, and will continue in it. We can ask what differentiates inanimate action as a species of inanimate doing, and what differentiates human action as a species of human doing, and what *if anything* differentiates action as a species of doing, while all the time keeping open the question whether the two kinds of action are action in the same sense. If we could give one differentia for action in general, that would lend support to the view that senses need not be distinguished. But even if we cannot, it seems to me that we must ask why all our five cases count as action and other kinds of doing do not.

A survey of the cases will show that several features suggest themselves as relevant to the classification of given cases as action, while at the same time their relevance varies over the range and resists explanation by any simple pattern. The first of these features is one which belongs to the given cases of human action, but could not be present in inanimate action. I will claim that it is part of the differentia of action by persons as a species of doing by persons. I will further claim that, with action as a genus, this feature is sufficient to differentiate that kind of action which various writers have sought as 'distinctively human action' and the like. At the same time, the exposition of this feature must be slightly complicated. I therefore devote the next section to it, and then in the following section attempt to relate this and the remaining features in some single account of action.

4.5 HUMAN ACTION AND RESPONSIBILITY

Let us note, then, some things in common among the cases of human action 2) to 5). On each occasion, the situation, including the abilities of the agent, was such that the question arose for him of whether or not to do that thing which in fact he did. As I have insisted before, this is a comment on the opportunities open to deliberation, and might be informatively addressed to the agent himself; it is not a comment on the agent's awareness of these opportunities, much less on his actual deliberation. But clearly some such further comment must be applicable; there are further, psychological features implied by the straightforward, unqualified reports of action which define these cases.

It seems evident that in each case not only does the person do something, and not only does the question of whether or not to do that thing arise for him, but also that these two facts are related in a particular way. Using the language of 1.2 and 1.3, we can recognize three kinds of case. Either the doing itself constitutes the settling of the question of what to do; or, where the settling of the question is a prior decision, resolution, or the like, the doing is the carrying out of that decision, resolution, etc.; or where the agent simply realizes that available considerations settle for him the question of what to do, the doing is the acting upon that realization. All three specifications presuppose that the question arose; their disjunction does not entail that deliberation or hesitation occurred, or any other incident than the doing itself. The disjunctive specification gives a relation in which the doing of the thing stands to the question of whether to do the thing, in the given four cases of human action. We can think of the doing as a fulfilling of the question of whether to do that thing, in the sense that it either is, or is the outcome of, a settling of the question. Since the point of view of the agent is that of the person for whom such a question arises, it is clear that in these cases of action there exists a point of view of the agent, and that the existence of this point of view is relevant in understanding how the action comes to occur.

The complex feature just described, which is present in the given cases, has an important role to play in the analysis of action. But in learning to define this role we must resist temptations both to oversimplify and to despair.

One is inclined to suggest that this feature is part of the differentia of human action as a species of human doing, i.e., that it provides a necessary but not sufficient condition for a person's doing something to be a case of action. But to this there is an obvious objection. A person's doing something can be action, even though it is neither the settling, nor the outcome of a settling, of the question of whether to do the thing, where the action is involuntary, unintentional, inadvertent, done accidentally, done by mistake, and so on. The putative necessary condition for action seems to fail for many of a familiar list of kinds of action in which the agent is not responsible for having done what he did. If a man steps back involuntarily as a car passes, the explanation of his action lies in the conditioning of certain reflexes and not in his preference for stepping back or his realization of the necessity of doing so. If he inadvertently flicks his cigarette ash onto my coat, so far from his action being his choice in the matter of whether to flick ash on me, the explanation of how he could have done it is that he failed to notice that, at that juncture, there was any question of his doing it. If he walks into someone's office by mistake, the question of whether to enter that office may not have occurred to him, he may have decided after deliberation to go back to his own, and his action will then have come about by a disorder in the execution of his decision whereby the decision is not carried out and the action is not decided on.

The list of such excuses is known to be long; there is no accepted theory which assigns them to a simple pattern or sets a limit to the list. In the face of such complexities, it might seem that the feature identified in our cases 2) to 5) provides at best a necessary condition for action for which the agent is responsible, and that the theory of action, from which we might hope for light on the obscurities of responsibility, is brought into unprofitable dependence on the theory of responsibility. The most we learn is that if the person's doing lacks this feature, then *either* it is not action *or* it is action but meets one of the many conditions for non-responsibility.

But this is to give in too easily. It is indeed to reverse the fruitful order of analysis, and we must reconsider the status of this feature as a necessary condition for human action, and the status of the excuses which release from responsibility.

It is natural to assume that involuntary action is action, that doing things inadvertently and doing things by mistake are kinds of action, and that nothing is a necessary condition of membership in the genus which is absent in members of a species. But these particular species of human action have differentiæ of an untypical sort. Each differentia is a defect in human action, not merely in the sense of being practically dangerous, unfortunate, or untoward, but in the sense of making the action a borderline case of human action. Some of the criteria for classifying an event as a human action fail to apply, or have faltering application, and it becomes correspondingly misleading to report the action without qualifying the action verb. The unqualified 'He did it' creates expectations which the adverbial excuses like 'involuntarily' and 'inadvertently' are needed to forestall. The role of such adverbs is therefore not merely to contribute further description of events which are straightforwardly cases of action, but to withdraw the implication that some standard feature is present, in cases where enough of the standard features are nevertheless present to justify calling the event an action. 'Involuntarily' attaches a *qualification* to the bare 'He did it'.

In the analysis of such a conceptual situation, it becomes inexpedient to attempt directly to state the necessary and sufficient conditions for human doing to be human action (of *any* kind). The first step is to give a necessary condition for straightforward or standard cases, and I think the feature whose merits we are considering contributes to a relatively elegant and fertile analysis when assigned this limited role. After that one can catalogue the qualifications which can be attached to the simple report of action. Finally, in confirmation of this strategy, and in the spirit of J. L. Austin's approach,[2] one might hope to exhibit the qualifications as lesions revealing the hidden anatomy of the normal case, and in particular revealing the complexities hidden in the stated necessary condition. Although I cannot undertake the analyses here, I suggest the theory that many of the excuses adverbially attached to reports of action both a) presuppose that the question of whether to do the thing did arise for the agent, and b) select one of the many kinds of breakdown whereby his doing what he did fails to be, or to be the outcome of, the settling of the question.

This view of human action is more conservative than that of Professor Hart[3] according to which the concept is 'defeasible' through being 'ascriptive'. On that view, since the force of 'He did it' is actually to ascribe responsibility, the concept of action is logically dependent on rules of conduct which determine when factual circumstances support or give good reasons for the ascription and when they defeat such an ascription. The defeasibility of the concept of responsibility thereby offers an explanation of how the concept of action can be correctly applicable under apparently simple circumstances, yet subject to such an unmanageable list of qualifications which 'reduce' the ascription. But the concept of human action still seems to me psychological rather than moral, and the role of the qualifications seems explicable without recourse to the ascriptivist view. Typically, an excuse like 'involuntarily' or 'by mistake' does not reduce the ascription of responsibility, but defeats it altogether,

2 J. L. Austin, 'A Plea for Excuses', in his *Philosophical Papers* (Oxford: Clarendon Press, 1961), pp. 127–8, 141–2.

3 H. L. A. Hart, 'The Ascription of Responsibility and Rights', *Aristotelian Society Proceedings* (1938–9) reprinted in A. G. N. Flew, ed, *Logic and Language*, first series (Oxford: Blackwell, 1951), sec III.

even though it remains true that the person did do the thing in question; what is 'reduced' is the full-bloodedness or nuclearity of his action in the array of human doings which count as action.

It would be consistent to add to a psychological theory of action an ascriptivist theory of responsibility on Hart's lines, according to which a set of behavioural criteria justified ascription of responsibility, subject to defeat by a variegated list of excuses. But even here I think that the leading principle of *prima facie* responsibility will not be behavioural in content, but will simply be the principle that a person is responsible for his actions. And I suspect that the rationale both of this principle and of the list of excuses which release from responsibility will be much illuminated by the psychological analysis of action. For responsibility seems to involve being appropriately called upon to justify having done something, in the sense of showing that there were adequate reasons for that particular settling of the question of whether to do it. If so, many of the criteria for responsibility would naturally turn upon whether one's action did in the first place represent the settling of that question.

The upshot of this discussion is that I claim the right, and announce the intention, of restricting the analysis to that range of human action which from the point of view of responsibility is straightforward, non-defective, and as it were nuclear. The analysis of responsibility, and of most of the psychological complexities about action, is thereby adjourned. But inside the favoured range we are left with a part of the differentia of human action within human doing. That the question of whether to do the thing arose, and that the doing was, or was the outcome of, a settling of the question, is a condition satisfied by our cases 2) to 5); and it seems to be, subject to our new limitation, a necessary condition for human doing to be human action.

Let us now consider a related but distinct approach to analysing human action *per genus et differentiam*. Take as genus not doing by some type of doer, nor yet doing by anything at all, but rather action by any agent whatever. Then let us ask, what species of the genus action is differentiated by the feature we have identified. Since the applicability of the concept demands an agent for whom questions can arise, we must at least have human action or some kind of human action. What kind of human action? By definition, for a human action to be of this kind, it is necessary and sufficient that it possess this feature. (We left open the possibility of further properties which would be necessary conditions of human *doing* being human *action*, and there are some in fact; but whatever these are they are already entailed by the joint specification of action as the genus and this feature as the differentia.) So the kind of human action in question is that straightforward and high-grade kind for which the agent is responsible. I observe that writers on ethics are often at pains to select something which they refer to as 'distinctively human action', or 'the action characteristic of moral agents' or 'action implying responsibility' or 'conscious action' or 'voluntary action' or just 'human action'. Relevance to ethics thus poses to philosophy of mind the problem of correctly identifying and analysing this kind of action. I suggest that the feature in question, viz., that the doing be, or be the outcome of, the settling of the question of whether to do that thing, provides the best solution to the problem of identification.

It is natural, and might eventually be desirable, to attempt a more ambitious solution. One might try to set out necessary and sufficient conditions for a natural phenomenon to be a case of 'distinctively human action', and to do so in strictly observational and behavioural terms, or at least in psychological terms the spectator's application of which is highly general and well understood. But we can be fore-warned by the evident difficulty of such an enterprise. Most at-tempts lack principles for ordering the welter of relevant psycho-logical concepts, such as consciousness, deliberation, intention and purpose. My strategy, which in effect identifies the kind of action by the existence of the point of view of the agent, does more than supply a principle for organizing such an account; it largely avoids the necessity for it altogether. Thus, simply by taking up the point of view of the agent, or by taking up a point of view defined as that of a spectator of an agent with such a point of view, one presup-poses the presence of any conditions necessary for the existence of the point of view of the agent. The agent must, for example, be a conscious agent, sometimes aware of what he is doing. But this awareness is an eye which sees the thing to be done without seeing itself. The agent deals with things and events in the natural world, including his body and what it does; but much that differentiates his action from other action is not in the agent's own visual field. The presuppositions of the existence of his point of view may be complicated and difficult to state, but we can get along without knowing what they are; the trick is to presuppose them. Of course some of them will be forced on our attention anyway, but it is not profitable to undertake a systematic analysis of them.

In this respect my approach is similar to that of Miss Anscombe in *Intention*. Her suggestion is that intentional actions are 'actions to which a certain sense of the question "Why?" is given application; the sense is of course that in which the answer, if positive, gives a reason for acting.' [4] In fact I think that the class of actions to which her question is given application, and the class of actions which has the feature I specify, are co-extensive, even if both are wider than the class of intentional actions. But in any case my way of picking out a kind of action follows hers in presupposing rather than specifying most of the psychological characteristics of the kind of action.

4.6 FURTHER FEATURES OF ACTION

The feature just discussed provides a necessary condition for human doing to be human action, and a necessary and sufficient condition for action to be of a certain important kind central to ethics. But it does not provide a sufficient condition for human doing to be human action. For there are some things a person does, and can (for example) have decided to do by way of settling the question of whether to do them, which do not count as action. These we encountered in 2.1, and categorized as *mental* doing in a sense explained there. For example, to turn one's attention to the consideration of a question, when there is no outward sign of one's doing so, is not action. It seems to be a further necessary condition for a person's doing to be action that there be some externally observable behaviour, some participation of the motor functions of his body, which is either logically or causally essential to doing that thing. Typically, there must be a motion of some kind in his body. A case of human action must simultaneously meet this physical,

4   G. E. M. Anscombe, *Intention* (Oxford : Blackwells, 1957), sec. 5.

behavioural condition and the psychological condition above.

Obvious difficulties confront the attempt to erect these conditions, either singly or jointly, into an account of action in general. By that I mean an account which gives the differentia of action as a species of doing, by giving necessary and sufficient conditions for A's doing to be A's action, whatever A is.

The psychological condition is the one most conspicuously not fulfilled by inanimate action, and one could extend it to our case 1) only at the cost of regarding the concept of inanimate action as anthropomorphic and confused. In Chapters 2 and 3 I think I have shown such a view to be both unnecessary and implausible. The behavioural condition is more promising, since it is more reasonable to suggest that physical motion is essential to action; the ideas of *activity* and being *active* might suggest a near identity between the concepts of motion and action, and a metaphorical status for that of mental activity. But obviously this will not do by itself on either the inanimate or the human side. One of the striking features of inanimate action is that sheer physical motion does not qualify; there must be an effect produced in something else. On the human side, the physical motion counts as motion (not action) of the body, but not necessarily as motion (and action) of the person. One task of any analysis is to bring out some additional condition, such as the psychological condition, which is needed for the motion to be counted as action of the person. Suppose that we were to use instead this motion of the person (which entails bodily motion), and thereby sweep both conditions under the single heading of the agent's motion. Then the analysis fits the nod of the head, case 5), exactly. But it offers no clue as to why, in case 2), the producing of an effect in the branch should be describable as an action of the person at all, much less why this description should be independent of any reference to the particular motion of the person. In case 3), in which the contracting of the lungs is not something the person does at all, it is even harder to connect the person's producing of an effect with his motion, and yet the producing of the effect is action.

Before considering how we might combine our two conditions, let us bring in other features of the cases. Cases 1) to 3) all involve an agent producing an effect in another thing by doing something (i.e., by a mode of operation). Where the agent is inanimate, this seems necessary and sufficient to make its doing into action. But we cannot extend such an analysis past the first three cases, for although the condition is sufficient to make human doing into action, as in cases 2) and 3), it is shown not to be necessary by 4), which is producing without a mode of operation, and by 5), which is just moving. If we weaken the condition by omitting the mode of operation, and thus cover 4), bodily movement is still not producing an effect in anything else. Furthermore, in case 2), where the producing of an effect on the branch is an action of the person's through the effect being attributable to his moving his hand, the mode of operation must itself be an action which the analysis will not cover.

But now a modification of this line might be combined with our two conditions for human action to suggest a more attractive theory. Perhaps action is necessarily a matter of producing a physical effect, of which motion would be typical; but in the case of human action, the motion is that of the body and the causal transaction is internal. Then for inanimate action, motion is produced in the thing acted on, and is produced by the agent's doing something for human action, motion is produced in the body, and is produced by the agent's doing something in his soul. For both cases, action is a transaction between two things, the second of which is made to move, but for human action the cause is a mental event. On this view, the psychological condition as stated is only the reflection of a condition that the physical movement be caused by a volition, choice, decision, or something of that kind.

The distinguished history of this theory is witness to its varied sources of power. Nevertheless, I think that enough has been done by Ryle, Wittgenstein, Anscombe and others to show that the fulfilment of the psychological condition cannot be represented as the presence of some psychological event or condition which stands in a causal relation to bodily movement. The objections concern both the impossibility of locating any decision, choice, 'volition' or the like for many cases of action, and the impossibility, where an action is in fact the carrying out of a decision or the like, of representing such a relation between decision and action as causal. I will not undertake to rehearse these objections now. Rather let me point out that such a theory, if tenable, would help to explain the fact that in both inanimate and human action a causal chain extending from the motion of the agent into successive effects on other things can give rise to new actions of the agent for new motions caused. Since my own account will preserve some affinity with this theory, particularly in this respect, it will further serve to disarm the theory by providing an alternative source of such an explanation.

I believe that the pieces of this puzzle can be fitted together only by a more complex analysis, the central idea of which is not causation but that of the attributability of effects to agents. This notion is at once wider than that of causation, through inclusion of non-causal attributability, and narrower, through restriction to agents rather than events or states of affairs. With the help of this idea, I will try to fit both inanimate action and human action, and thereby to fit action in general, into the theory of attributability. The theory of attributability can be regarded simply as a version, adapted for this purpose, of the theory of explanation.

4.7 SCHEMATIC ACCOUNT

The account which we are about to develop in the next five sections is meant to be adequate for the representative cases of action under examination. It will be obvious that there are many clear cases of human action, including many of particular interest to ethics, which do not fit the analysis. There can be no question therefore of offering necessary and sufficient conditions for any doing to be action. But I think it is reasonable to be guided by the conviction that our five favoured cases are nuclear cases of action, and to approach the inclusive task by finding an analysis for them and then considering what modifications or additions are needed to reach the peripheral cases. Progress from the first approximation could take a variety of forms. One might find that the analysis provided sufficient but not necessary conditions for action, and proceed to locate other sets of conditions to take their place in a disjunction of sets of sufficient conditions. For example, where this analysis covers the producing of effects on things, one might disjoin with it an analysis which covers the bringing about of states of affairs, and another (much more complex) which covers the getting of people to do things, and so on. Again, one might learn something from a precise delineation of the region within which any given set of sufficient conditions were also necessary conditions for action. Eventually one might hope for an account which would yield the partial analyses and also explain their limitations and interrelations. Only then could one fully vindicate a claim for the primacy of the present analysis. But I think that the fruits of an analysis which gets as far as relating inanimate action, bodily movement, and simple manipulation will be enough to lend the claim some support.

Let us fasten on two ideas which will be threads running through the whole account. The first is one which figured in the previous review of the five cases, namely the idea of a motion or change in a physical thing. It is typically motion that is in question. Such a motion, whether of sand, branch, hand, arm or head, is involved in each of the cases, and it is a publicly observable phenomenon. With respect to this phenomenon let us take up the point of view of a spectator. With regard to human action, the points of view of the agent and of the spectator are points of view on one and the same thing, the person's action. Nothing which we learn looking at action from the spectator's point of view can be false from the agent's point of view (though the question may not arise for the agent); and by the same token there is no bar in principle to discovering that the ground plan of the concept of action is laid down by concepts which seem characteristically spectator's concepts. Such is the second of our two ideas, that of something being attributable to something else, where this attributability is such as to constitute at least some kind or degree of explanation. Let us call this the idea of explanatory attributability. One interest characteristic of an observer is that of understanding, or being able to explain, the phenomena he encounters. We are able to place the concept of action within the theory of explanatory attributability because we are able to place all our cases of action among the occasions on which the spectator observes the motions occurring in nature with understanding, in that he knows what they are attributable to.

Schematically, these two ideas combine as follows to yield an analysis of action for our cases. A motion or change in a physical thing B, when it is attributable to something, can be called an effect on B. When the effect on B is attributable to another thing A, we have a case of A's action, and A is an agent. When A is an inanimate physical thing, the effect on B is causally attributable to A; what A is said to do is to produce the effect on B; and A's producing this effect is a case of inanimate action. When A is a person, the effect on B is attributable to A but not causally, or not purely causally. What A is said to do is in some cases to produce the effect on B, namely in those cases where the attributability is partly causal; in other cases, A is said merely to move or change in some way. Whichever sort of thing A is said to do, it is a case of human action.

The most difficult part of this schema is to show the way in which effects on physical things are attributable to persons without this relation being a causal one. The assumption that such attributability must be causal would turn this analysis into some version of the theory of volitions already rejected. On the other hand, an adequate account of the relevant non-causal explanatory attributability would open the way to securing most of the advantages for which causal theories have been valued.

We need first to consider some features of explanatory attributability in general (4.8). Then, in the following two sections (4.9 – 4.10), we can add some of the specific features of inanimate action, and thereby discharge the task of exhibiting more fully the way in which inanimate action is a species of natural causation. Then we can develop the account of the non-causal attributability of physical motion and change to persons (in 4.11). Finally by combining the two branches of the analysis we can hope (in 4.12) to discharge the task of exhibiting the naturalness and the mutual relations of the differentiae of inanimate and human action, and we can take stock of progress toward a single differentia for action in general.

4.8 EXPLANATORY ATTRIBUTABILITY

We speak of attributing properties to things and views to authors, as well as of attributing effects to causes. Whatever it may be for a property to be attributable to a thing, or a view to be attributable to an author, it does not seem that the relation necessarily contributes anything at all to the explanation of the property or of the view. For the present purpose, the only relevant uses of the word are those in which, on the contrary, to attribute one thing to a second, in the sense of saying that the first is attributable to the second, is to attempt to provide, in whole or in part, an explanation of the first thing. It is to these uses that we are confining ourselves from here on, under the heading of explanatory attributability.

What sorts of things can be thus attributable to what sorts of things? The variety on both sides is very wide. Instead of reviewing it, let me offer an indication of its extent embedded in the following theory of the main structure of the concept. Anything's being the case is attributable to something else's being the case, without logical restriction on the form of what is said to be the case; for the ground plan of this concept of attributability is given by the form 'This is so because that is so'. This is the simplest way to attribute the first thing's being so to the second thing's being so. The restrictions on what can be attributed to what are no narrower than the restrictions on the content of the two clauses, being indeed founded on them. So we can have :

> The rock is hot because the sun has been shining on it. The bridge collapsed because a girder was too light. It's wrong because it discriminates on racial grounds. He thinks she is a Catholic because he knows she is French. He thinks it's true because he can't face the alternatives.

Each of these attributes something to something else. We can identify the two things without committing ourselves about their logical type by staying close to the same forms of speech; e.g., we can say that the rock's being hot is attributed to the sun's having been shining on it. There seem also in various cases to be various identifications available on either side; e.g., we can speak of the condition of the rock; the action of the sun; an event, namely the collapse of the bridge; a property of a thing, namely the size of the girder. In addition, with one curious qualification, what we are talking about on both sides of the 'because' are facts. Thus the rock's being hot is attributable to the fact that the sun has been shining on it; and this entails that the fact that the rock is hot is at least partly explained by the same fact. The qualification required is that, while the relation of attributability entails that the first fact is partly explained by the second fact, there is for some reason a straining of logical type in saying that the *fact* is itself *attributable* to anything: 'the rock's being hot' is better than 'the fact that the rock is hot', as a way of identifying that which is said to be attributable to something else.

With this qualification, I am willing to argue that the term 'fact' is available on both sides throughout this whole range of cases, including the moral one. But I doubt that this versatility of the term is portentous; it is just that facts have more idiosyncrasies than is often supposed. The relation of the fact idiom to the vocabulary of events, properties, conditions, and the like is a complex problem which I will avoid as far as possible.

Evidently an attribution of this kind gives the reason why something is so, and not merely the reason for saying it is so. The distinction needs mentioning, since each of the examples above may have associated with it a form of justification or argument which might be confused with it. Where the attribution must be punctuated 'q because p', the justification or argument may be and usually is punctuated 'q, because p'. I trust the distinction between the two forms is familiar enough.

There is no room here to develop this aspect of the concept of attributability. But it would evidently be in the spirit of most theories of explanation to trace a connexion between 'q because p' and 'q, because p' and between the latter in turn and 'If p, then q'. My interpretation of Hume amounts to saying that one of his fundamental and least celebrated insights was that attributability is partly analysable in terms of inferability. Actually, I think it holds generally that the statement that *q because p* entails that the given particular circumstances to which this applies are such that *q if and only if p*. Certain problems in the analysis of causation which turn on assigning the right role to such assertions of necessary and sufficient conditions are really more general problems about the structure of attributability of any kind. In particular, it is evident that 'q and p, and q if and only if p' cannot exhaust the analysis of 'q because p', since the former relates 'p' and 'q' symmetrically and the latter asymmetrically. Something must be added to the analysis to determine which explains which. But this is an unsolved problem in the general theory of attributability, and not merely in the theory of causation.

We must turn in a different direction for those developments of the account of attributability which are relevant to the present analysis. So far, that *to* which anything is attributable has been an event, condition, state of affairs, or something else whose structure is analogously related to the propositional structure of a fact. For the theory of action we must attend to kinds of attributability which are parasitic on this kind, being in a limited range of cases derivable from it, and in which it is a physical thing or person to which something is attributable. For attributability to a physical thing we can now turn to the account of inanimate action as a species of natural causation.

4.9 *CAUSAL ATTRIBUTABILITY AND INANIMATE ACTION*

For causal attributality we can lay down one restriction on logical types: it will require something empirical at both ends. More is obviously needed for an analysis of the notion of cause, but it is not clear that anything further needs to be said about the possible types to which must belong the report of the cause and the report of the thing caused, at least until one comes to the relations between the two. Taking each by itself, a cause may be an event or the condition of an object or a relation between objects or the absence of a property, and so on, and things of any of these types can be attributed to a cause.

Next let us restrict our attention to inanimate nature. At the cause end of the relation, this restriction is simply one step towards our present intention of locating inanimate action. At the other end of the relation, we are restricting ourselves to inanimate nature with respect to the things which can be attributed to causes; we are thus excluding cases in which something physical causes a person to do something, whether what he does is to believe or to hiccough or to sleep or to run. The reason for this restriction is that the notion of causing a person to do something, where this latter is high-grade, responsible action, is clearly very different from that of causing a physical effect in a person, and yet it is difficult both to provide an analysis and to sort out the intermediate cases. Collingwood rightly gave special treatment to what he called sense I of 'cause'[5] as in 'The change in the weather caused him to turn back', and there are analogous uses of 'make', 'bring', 'force', 'compel', 'induce' and so on. But so far from agreeing that these ideas are fundemental in the analysis, I think their complexity and their affinity with metaphor justify us in postponing for the time being any attempt to include them in the analysis.

Out of the many remaining things which causes can cause, let us now select those which can be called *effects*. This concept of effect is the second of the two identified in 2.2, where the examples given were conveyed by the intransitive or absolute uses of verbs like 'move', 'bend', 'warm' and 'open'. For example, one effect that could be produced on a billiard ball would be that it moved; on a branch, that it bent. Alternatively we may speak of the *motion* of the ball and the *bending* of the branch as effects produced. To iden- tify such things as effects is of course not merely to speak of them as things which could in principle be attributed to something else, but as things which are in fact known to be attributable. The main implied restriction of type on things which can be effects in this sense I stated in 2.2 by saying that effects must be *on* something. Thus, under our present restrictions, the fact being attributed must be the fact that some spatio-temporal thing did something (e.g., moved or bent).

Effects which have been produced in things, even if they can all be attributed to facts, can also be attributed to things of a variety of types; in other words they can be attributed to facts of a variety of forms. For example, the freezing of pipes might be attributed to the *coldness of the night*, or to *a window's being open*, or to *the lack of a furnace*. Such causes are hard to categorize; they seem to be kinds of condition, state of affairs, or circumstances. It is neverthe- less correct to say that they have effects, e.g., to say that the effect on the pipes of the coldness of the night, or of the window's being open, or of the lack of a furnace, was that the pipes froze. It is also possible to attribute effects to events, while yet not attributing them to events which consist of the action of things. For example, the effect on a person of *a sudden increase in blood flow* to the digestive

5 R. G. Collingwood, *An Essay on Metaphysics* (Oxford : Clarendon, 1940), p. 290.

organs might be that he felt faint, although we could not say that the blood or any other such thing made him feel faint. (*Lack of oxygen* hardly qualifies as a thing that can act.) However, the very difficulty of thinking of such examples impresses one with the central position of those cases in which an effect on one thing is attributed to an event which consists of another thing's doing something, where the doer, while it need not be a physical object (like a stone), must be some kind of spatio-temporal thing (the wind, the tide, the heat of the sun), and where the doing must be moving or changing, or, itself, acting on another thing. (Cf. end of 2.4)

Let us then consider cases where we can say that B did something because A did something, where this is a causal attribution, and where the doing is of this restricted kind. Now let us consider the relation between the form

B did y because A did x,

and the following forms:

A made B do y by doing x,
A produced (a) y-ing in B by doing x.

For example, where the sand moved because the log pushed on it, we have the forms: the log made the sand move by pushing on it, and the log produced motion in the sand (or a motion of the sand) by pushing on it. These forms notably differ from the first in structure, in that we now have a single main verb which takes the agent as subject and the thing acted on as some kind of verbal or prepositional object, and relegates to a modifying phrase what I have called (2.3) the agent's mode of operation. At the same time they are closely related in meaning. The latter two forms clearly entail the first. In order to obtain an entailment in the other direction, however, we have to conjoin with the first form a restricting condition. For there is a type of case in which B did *y* because A did *x*, and yet it follows only that A *let* B do *y*, or in some other way completed the necessary conditions for B doing *y*, without *making* B do *y*. For example, in explaining the collapse of the bridge we could attribute the fall of the structure to the fact that the particular girder *buckled*, and this would be an attribution of the first form. Yet evidently it was rather the weight of the structure which made it fall; or if one prefers, without anything making it fall, it simply is the case that things fall given the conditions created by the buckling of the girder.

The exclusion of such cases is not arbitrary from the point of view of our analysis. For it seems evident that where 'because' does not yield 'makes', the force of the attribution is different, and in a certain respect parasitic upon that of simpler cases. The fall of the bridge is attributable to the buckling of the girder *only because* the fact of its buckling brings the effect under an explanation which covers the falling of supported and unsupported objects generally and is also available in this case; it is just that in this case the standard explanation, that the bridge fell by its own weight (as unsupported objects do), can be taken for granted, whereas the change in the girder is the particular fact needed to explain how this standard explanation is applicable. So the cases we need to exclude are those in which it is the case that B did y because A did x only because the fact that A did x explains the applicability of another and more basic explanation of why B did y. To exclude such cases is to confine ourselves to cases in which the statement that B did y because A did x provides, itself, the basic explanation of why B did y.

Given this restriction, we can say then that the second two forms have the same force as the first two, but differ from it in structure. So what they provide is a way of stating the original attribution in the form of a report of what A did. It will have to be a report of what *A* did *to B*. 'Make' and 'produce' offer general devices for casting attributions in this form. There are also the transitive uses of verbs which in their intransitive uses can report pure effects, like 'move', 'bend', 'warm', 'open'. As I noted in 2.2 'move' (transitive) can be analysed as 'make move' (intransitive). In addition, there are many special words and idioms, like 'cut', 'raise', 'deflect', 'enlarge', 'push along', 'hold down'.

A causal attribution in this form reports the *action* of one thing on another. The thing A is thereby given the status of *agent*. The report that A did one thing, namely, x, is replaced, in the light of knowledge of the effects on B of this event, by the report of a new thing which A did, namely make B do y, whose internal structure is founded on the relation of attributability of one event to another. The peculiarity of this structure is that the effect is no longer attributed to *A's doing* x but simply to A, and the original doing of x is relegated to a modifier telling *how* A made B do *y*.

This modifier can be omitted; it is apparent therefore that we have here a new and derivative kind of attributability. The effect is now attributable *to A*, in the sense of being attributable merely to the *action* or to *agency* of A, without reference to the whole fact to which the effect is in the old sense attributable. Although there must always exist what I have called the mode of operation of A, all explicit reference to it can disappear in favour of the identification of an agent as the sole factor to be offered in explanation of the effect in B. The descriptive role of the report becomes dominant over the explanatory role, which is only partially filled.

In this section we have arrived at the concept of inanimate action by a new route; we have sought out its place within a general theory of attributability. We took as highest genus attributions of the form 'q because p', and approached our concept by successive delimitations. First we selected causal attributions, with the implied restriction to empirical facts at both ends, and then those causal attributions which concern inanimate nature. Then among the things attributable to such causes we selected effects, and those effects which involve a spatio-temporal thing's *doing* something in a narrowed sense. Among the causes to which such effects are attributable, we selected first events, and then those events which consist of another spatio-temporal thing's similarly *doing* something. Causal attribution in the inanimate realm which pairs two such facts might be said to imply the attribution of an effect to inanimate action; it entails attribution of the effect in a further, derived sense, where the form of the attribution is explicitly a report that the agent-thing *produced* the effect in the thing acted on, or *made* it do the thing being explained. This construction coupled with the entailment by the causal attribution together sketch an analysis of inanimate action.

4.10 THE RELATIVE SIMPLICITY OF ACTION

According to the foregoing analysis, the fact that an inanimate agent A acted on B can be abstracted from a fact of a particular form, viz., that *q because p*, where the fact that p is the fact that A did something, and the fact that q is the fact that B did something. Attributions of the form *q because p* are simple, relative to the degrees of complexity which the explanation of facts can sometimes attain. This simplicity entails that reports of inanimate action, considered as they occur in the context of attempts to understand and explain natural phenomena, and as they contribute to that attempt such explanatory force as they have, are also relatively simple. Where no such simplicity is attainable in the explanations of why things happen as they do, it will not be possible to pick out agents and to explain effects by attributing them to those agents; and conversely, where it is possible to apply the concepts of agent and action, a certain simplicity in the natural phenomena is presupposed. It is therefore worth formulating, at least roughly, two of the respects in which attribution of this type is simple.

First, both the fact that q and the fact that p are restricted to the form *A did* x (or *B did* y), where A and B are identifiable physical things. Action thus belongs at a level of generality between that of the concept Hume purported to analyse, i.e., causation in general, and that of the concept he came close to analysing, i.e., mechanical force in particular. For his specification of contiguity in place seems to require not merely two physical things, but in particular two physical things which can be said to touch. Inanimate action is less specific a notion, but does require identifiable physical things. This specification is vaguely formulated, but I think it is unnecessary for present purposes to make it much more precise. Let us say that a wave in water qualifies, though marginally, as an identifiable physical thing, while the set of papers strewn on my desk does not qualify at all. This restriction excludes many familiar kinds of causal attribution. We can explain a change in the weather, or the distribution of smallpox, or a diffraction pattern; none of these is an effect on an identifiable physical thing, but requires a more complex description. We can explain effects in terms of such things; but again each thing requires a more complex description that that of an identifiable thing which does something. There may be a grammatically simple subject-predicate form (like 'The weather is getting cold'), but the subject term then covers up the physical complexity.

The second kind of simplicity is reflected in the syntactical simplicity of 'q because p'. Actually, wherever we can correctly give such a simple explanation, it is always the case that q because p *only because r, s,* and *t,* and therefore it is also the case that: q because p, r, s, and t. In other words, where we are able to attribute the fact that q to the fact that p, the simplicity of our attribution depends on the fact that certain standing conditions are fulfilled. Where 'q because p' is a direct application of an empirical law, these will include the conditions under which the law holds. A situation in which an effect which we wish to explain can be correlated by a known empirical law with the action of an identifiable physical thing is scientifically and practically speaking a simple situation.

There is a consequence for any case in which causal explanation of an effect on a thing requires reference to a complex situation, and where the relevant description of the situation, in so far as it involves identifiable physical things, requires reference to many of them and to the relations among them. In such a case the complexity of the explaining facts precludes the attribution of the effect to any physical agent. We may take an example from a field which will shortly become relevant. Let us suppose the contraction of a muscle to be attributable to the amplification of a pattern of excitation in the cerebral cortex under the influence of a frequency of stimulation from another part of the cortex. Then the complexity of this account would preclude attribution of this effect on the muscle to any physical agent.

4.11 *NON-CAUSAL ATTRIBUTABILITY TO PERSONS*

The theory which I have offered analyses inanimate action in terms of explanatory attributability to physical things, and analyses this attributability to *things* as an aspect of attributality *to motion or change in things.* Thus action itself is regarded as an aspect of such attributability. For the report that A made B do y is a selection from a certain vantage point of information contained in the full attribution, viz., that B did y because A did x; and when offered alone it nevertheless implies the obtainability of the rest of the explanation. That is why it is a necessary condition of attributability of an effect to an inanimate agent that that agent have some mode of operation or other. It is the existence of this necessary condition which makes the concept of inanimate action intelligible.

Let us now turn to the attributability of physical motion or change to persons. It is clear from our case 2) of action, in which someone breaks a branch by pressing down with his hand, that attributability to some mode of operation of the agent, which for inanimate agents is necessary and sufficient for attributability to the agent, is at any rate sufficient for attributability to the person. But we have already seen from case 4), of blowing, that it is not a necessary condition. More important, we have noticed that case 2) depends on the mode of operation being itself action, and that this action will include sheer bodily movement like case 5), of nodding the head. Clearly for bodily movement there is no question of a mode of operation. So both direct producing of effects and bodily movement show that the availability of a mode of operation is not a necessary condition of the attributability of motion to a person. Therefore if we wonder how it can be attributable to a person, there is no answer on the lines that it is simply an aspect of attributability to a kind of event, where the latter attributability is intelligible on Humean lines. I think this desire to find a mode of operation to fill this role is one of the motives for postulating volitions as the causes of bodily movement. Our problem is to make attributability to a person intelligible by some other route.

It might be suggested that there is no problem, about bodily movement at least, on the ground that when a person is said to move his hand or nod his head the motion of his body is attributed to him in a quite distinct and non-explanatory sense. Certainly it is incorrect to say that the motion is attributed to the person's action, and somewhat stretched to say that it is attributed to his agency or to say that he makes it occur. It is rather that the motion is the content of his action. Since his hand and head are parts of him, when he moves them he moves. It might seem that no more is involved if we say that he moves when they move, than is involved if we say that a tree moves when its branch waves in the wind, or that a stone moves when it rolls on the ground. These are in one sense attribution of motion to stone, tree, or person; but as the two reports are purely descriptive, perhaps the third is also.

We must grant (as we did in 2.6) that a person can move in exactly the same way as an inanimate object, e.g., in falling. A man can also be said to move, just as can a sail or coil of rope, in virtue of some part moving, typically when that part is displaced in an un-obvious way. In such cases his motion is not action any more than it would be if he were an inanimate object. But most of the time, when a man is said to move, this is a report of action, and then the force of the report is not merely descriptive of observable phy-sical motion. What is usually true for 'He moved' is always true for many specific reports of motion like 'He moved his hand' or 'He stood up' or 'He crouched'. The fact is that such reports of a person moving do contribute to an explanation of why the parts of his body moved. The reports are explanatory attribution, though of an attenuated kind. For it is intelligible and informative to say that a person's hand moved *because* he moved it.

To appreciate the force of this 'because', compare two different explanations of a glass being spilled on the floor: a) the glass tipped because his foot pushed it, and b) the glass tipped because he pushed it with his foot (where there are no qualifications like 'accidentally'). Obviously (b) entails (a). But (b) says more in explanation of the event, and yet adds nothing to the causal explanation of the glass's tipping. Its extra explanatory force is like the whole force of the 'because' in question.

To say that a person moved his hand, and not merely that his hand moved, is at least to bring the observable phenomena under a general category of explanation, that of explanation by reference to his soul. In other words, it is to bring the phenomena under a type of explanation which is applicable only to animate things, and only to animate things of the human grade of complexity. But further, it is to imply a more specific restriction on the type of explanation that could be given. We can regard the soul as a set of capacities and tendencies more or less integrated with each other. To assign something the person does to one particular faculty of the soul is to bring it under the heading of an exercise of some capacity or a manifestation of some tendency, and thereby to establish more specifically the type of explanation which will be appropriate. In saying that a person moved his hand, we not merely invoke the soul as the general field of explanation for the motion of his hand, we assign the motion to the exercise of a particular capacity the person has. Of course this capacity will include some sort of capacity to move his hand. Now some plants and most animals have capacities of various sorts to move parts of themselves. But to say of a person simply that he moved his hand invokes the presumption that in doing so he exercised a capacity to move himself such as is characteristic of human beings. The capacity is the one whose exercises are that kind of doing which (as I noted in 4.5) has been sought under the headings of 'distinctively human action', 'voluntary action', and the like. The identification which I proposed for that kind of action yields a corresponding identification of the capacity we now seek. To ascribe this capacity to a creature is to say that it is a creature for whom questions of what to do can arise; that it can consider such questions, and either settle them or realize that considerations settle them; and that it comes in this way to do some of the things it does. Accordingly, to attribute the motion of his body to a person is to imply that the motion is to be understood through the explanations of exercises of this capacity.

For such an account to work, it will have to turn out that, when the spectator assigns a movement of a person's body to an exercise of this capacity, he thereby assigns it to a recognizable and important type of explanation. In other words, the exercises of this capacity will have to be a range of phenomena open to such a type of explanation. But clearly this is so. The point of view of the agent is the organizing principle of those explanations of what people do which proceed by giving their reasons, intentions, purposes, and the like. In Chapter I we began to sketch the way in which the justifications for doing something can be organized from the point of view of the agent. Roughly speaking, the spectator explains human action by understanding the justifications that might be available from the point of view of the agent, and by understanding the many ways in which actual deliberation or conduct deviates from that rational deliberation and conduct which the spectator reconstructs from the agent's point of view.

Actual explanations of this type are abundantly familiar. Much could be said about the variety of structures that are common, but much has been said, and a few examples will do here. Granting that the hand moved because the person moved it, it may be that he moved his hand: with the intention of picking something up, in order to avoid being stepped on, because he wanted this, because he feared that, because something was about to happen, because he mistakenly thought it was. In each case, he did what he did *because* he intended, wanted, thought something. So in each case we can analyse the explanation as asserting the attributability of his action to psychological facts about him. This attributability, though explanatory, is not causal. The question we must raise is that of the relation between this attributability of a person's action to psychological facts about him and the attributability of motion in his body to him.

So far I have said only that to attribute the motion of a person's hand to the person is to lay down a type of explanation as the appropriate type. We have just noted that an explanation of this type, when actually available, proceeds by non-causal relations between the action and psychological facts about the person, this being the sense in which the explanation lies in the soul. But I have not said that there must actually be an explanation of this appropriate type. Here, once again, the analogy with causal attributability might tempt us to go too far. Just as it is a necessary condition for causal attributability of an effect to an agent that there be a mode of operation, i.e., that there be some thing the agent does and that the effect be attributable to the fact that he does it, so we might think it a necessary condition for attributability of bodily movements to a person that there be some psychological fact about the person and that the movement, as an aspect of the person's making the movement, be attributable to that psychological fact. In cases where there is such an explanation of the person's action, the condition will in fact be satisfied. But if we accepted the view that the condition is necessary for attributability of the movement to the person, we would be committed to saying that the motion of the hand is attributable to the person only when there is an explanation of his moving his hand. In other words, we would be committed to saying that there is a psychological explanation of the appropriate kind for each action. But clearly a person may just do something for no reason at all. And with irrational action, which is actually contrary to reason, part of the force of calling the action irrational is to imply the impossibility of reconstructing even the agent's bad reasons for what he did, and to hand the action over to such causal explanation as a psychologist may hope to find. But doing something for no reason, or doing something irrational, can very well be action to which explanation by reasons is appropriate. It can very well be an exercise, however unpropitious a one, of the capacity to settle questions of what to do. An exercise of free will can be capricious or irrational (although if it degenerates far enough in the scale of irrationality, its status may be undermined.) Successful explanation by reasons will of course establish *a fortiori* the appropriateness of explanation of that type, but it is only the appropriateness which is entailed by the attributability of bodily movement to a person.

It is evident then that such attributability is doubly attenuated. This attenuation is not due to the attributability being non-causal, for that is simply an independent and equally respectable kind. It is due, first, to the form of attributability to an agent rather than to an event, condition, or the like; as in the case of causal attributability to an agent, it constitutes less than a complete explanation. The attenuation is due, second, to the fact that it does not entail the existence of the full explanation, but only the appropriateness of such an explanation. However, since in the normal range of human action such explanations are actually available, this second attenuation is not very noticeable.

So far, in describing this kind of attributability, we have kept to cases of bodily movement like those of hand 2) and head 5). Bodily movement which, like the contraction of the lungs 4), is not entailed in the doing of anything which can present itself to deliberation, and which may be unknown to the agent, requires an extended treatment. To the agent the difference is decisive. The question of doing the one thing can be deliberated about, that of doing the other simply cannot. But from the point of view of explaining what happens, the difference scarcely matters. We are accustomed anyway to the realization that when the agent moves his hand, muscles contract and a thousand things unknown to the agent go on which are in fact indispensable to the occurrence of those particular motions which logically constitute his hand's moving. Similarly, when the agent manipulates other things, he makes many indispensable bodily movements of which he could be aware but in fact is not aware. The agent's capacity to do various things at will is in fact dependent on the organized functioning of his body, and when we explore, in physiology, learning theory, and the like, the ways in which this functioning underlies the voluntary powers, there seems no reason to assign a radically disparate role to those bodily movements which are definitionally related to the intentions of the agent. Thus comparable considerations are relevant to establishing any of the following explanations:

> *His hand moved because he moved it.*
> *His biceps muscle contracted because he moved his hand.*
> *His lungs contracted because he blew on the book.*
> *His foot moved back because he chopped at a higher branch.*
> *These back muscles tightened because he turned to the left of the parking lot.*
> *This set of nerves was activated because he moved the ink-bottle.*

This is a kind of explanation in which, roughly speaking, some aspect of a person's action is explained by reference to the very fact that it is an aspect of his action. I do not pretend to develop an account of the basis of such explanation, but I think it is clear at least that the basis of the explanation could be regarded as having two levels. On one, a bodily process is shown to be physically or logically a part of the producing of some particular physical event. On the next, that physical event, whether it is inside or outside the body, is shown to be related to the intentions, purposes, reasons, and the like, of the agent. His moving his hand is just the degenerate case in which the bodily event to be explained provides the actual content of the agent's intention, and no causal stage of the explanation is needed. Similarly, working in the other direction, we can regard 'His hand moved because he moved it' as a degenerate case of 'The axe moved because he moved his hand', where the effects produced in the world are contracted until they lie wholly within an intentional bodily movement; here the causal relations between body and environment drop out of the account, as previously the causal relations within the body dropped out of the account.

This account gains some confirmation from the existence of the stretched sense of 'make happen' which I have acknowledged here and in 2.7. This is the sense in which a person, in raising his hand, makes happen the many physiological events which are involved but which are unknown to him. One is tempted to say such a thing at all because, in general, the use of 'make' tends to follow that of 'attributable', and here, the physiological events are in one way attributable to the person's action and thus to him. At the same time, the sense is stretched, and the use uncomfortable, because the attributability is of this complex and indirect sort, in a field which is nearly pre-empted by the more full-blooded relations of attributability.

4.12 DIFFERENTIÆ

Let us now draw together the analysis of inanimate action and that of the selected cases of human action, and consider to what extent the concept of attributability allows us to see something in common and something different in the two kinds of action.

Let u be a thing which an inanimate thing (A) does. Then according to our analysis, the following complex condition is sufficient for A's doing u to be inanimate action, and necessary and sufficient for A's doing u to be inanimate action on an inanimate thing. The condition is that the statement that A does u be at least partly analysable as the conjunction of two statements which concern a second physical thing (B) and a kind of moving or changing (doing y), namely the statements i) that B does y, and ii) that B's doing y is causally attributable to A's moving or changing. For example, the log's pushing the sand along satisfies this condition, since the report that the log did this is partly analysable as saying i) that the sand moved, and ii) that the sand's moving was causally attributable to the log's moving or changing. The second part (ii) in turn entails that there is some particular thing of this kind (call it x) which A does and that B's doing y is causally attributable to A's doing x (e.g., to the log's pushing on the sand). In this particular sample, it happens the rest of the analysis would include the specification of x. In summary, the condition for A's doing u to be action is that, for some appropriate B and y, A's doing u be partly analysable as the conjunction of i) B's doing y and ii) there being some appropriate x such that B's doing y is causally attributable to A's doing x. Conjunct ii) of course entails that B's doing y is attributable simply to A.

Now let u be a thing which a person (A) does. According to our analysis, we can bring the representative cases of human action 2) to 5) under a complex condition parallel to the one just given. This will be a sufficient condition for A's doing u to be an unqualified, non-defective case of human action, and a necessary and sufficient condition for A's doing u to belong to some nuclear category of human action not yet otherwise identified.

The condition is that the statement that A does u be at least partly analysable as the conjunction of two statements which concern, once again, a physical thing (B) which moves or changes in some way (does y), where B is distinguishable from the person A. This last specification for B includes of course axes and bits of wood, but it also includes the body and its parts. There is no difficulty about counting the parts of the body, but I also wish to count the person's body, as a whole, as distinguishable from the person. Although I think it is correct to say that a person has physical characteristics, and is a physical thing, it must also be correct to say that his body is a physical thing distinguishable from him; for B will be distinguishable from A if something can be true of one and false or absurd of the other. (Cf. the way in which the surface of an object is distinguishable from the object.) Given this range of possible values for 'B', the condition requires there to be a value which yields an analysis of the statement that A does u into the conjunction of two statements: i) that B does y, and ii) that B's doing y is attributable to A. The attributability asserted in conjunct ii) is that attributability to persons discussed above; the basis of it may or may not be partly causal, but it must be at least partly non-causal. The formulation therefore covers all our cases; this we can exhibit as follows, taking each case as A doing u. The breaking of the branch of the tree will serve as B doing y, for we can analyse cases 2) and 3) as the branch's breaking and this being causally attributable directly (case 2) or indirectly (case 3, via the axe) to the motion of the hand, where the motion of the hand is non-causally attributable to the agent. In case 4), the air moves and its motion is causally attributable to the contraction of the lungs, which in turn is non-causally attributable to the agent. In case 5), the head moves and its motion is non-causally attributable to the agent. In summary, the condition for A's doing u to be action is that for some appropriate B and y, A's doing u be

at least partly analysable as the conjunction of i) B's doing y and
ii) B's doing y being attributable to A.

We may now take stock of the two analyses on hand. The first
merely codifies the account of inanimate action given throughout,
and evidently preserves the differentia already given for inanimate
action as a species of inanimate doing. The second analysis uses a
particular attenuated form of non-causal attributability to relate the
two aspects of the previously given differentia of human action.
These were, first, that the doing be, or be the outcome of, the settling
of the question of whether to do that thing; and second, that there be
some externally observable behaviour which is either logically or
causally essential to doing that thing. The second is provided for
since, by our analysis, either B's doing y is itself the observable behaviour or else, being outside the body, it must be causally attributable to some bodily motion or change (which is in turn non-causally
attributable to the person). The first is provided for, since the required attributability must be, at least in part, of the non-causal kind
described; and according to that description, it consists in the *appropriateness* of explaining what the agent does by reference to his
intentions, reasons for doing the thing, and the like. But the condition
for appropriateness of such explanation is precisely that the doing
be, or be the outcome of, the settling of the question of whether to
do the thing. So the analyses account for both the observed
differentiæ.

Comparing the two analyses, I think it must be acknowledged that
they show a very close formal similarity. But it is equally clear that
this similarity of structure, which allows almost the same form of
words to serve for both, is obtained by a rather contrived specification of two kinds of attributability. That these specifications, however contrived, should yield a single form of words to cover all of
our representative cases of action 1) to 5), does something by itself
to make them interesting. But the question arises whether there is
some further point of view from which they could be seen not to be
arbitrary or tendentious.

If there is, we will be in a stronger position to conjecture that
action in general is, to put it roughly, a matter of the attributability
of phenomena to things, where the typical phenomenon is motion
and the typical things are particles and people. The question of how

many senses the word 'action' has would then turn in part on how many senses the word 'attributability' has. One reason for regarding the word as having a single sense is its obviously close relation to the idea of explanation. As things of many kinds can explain a fact without requiring us to distinguish senses of 'explain', so bases of many kinds might support an assertion of attributability without requiring us to distinguish senses of the word. But this is a further issue, best judged perhaps in the light of the attempt to extend the present line of analysis into the bringing about of states of affairs, the achieving of results and other such complex domains of human action. For the time being, let us consider just the possibility of showing that the common structure of the analyses given so far is not an arbitrary or tendentious construction.

4.13 EXPLANATION BY CAUSES AND BY REASONS

It is usually a dark undertaking to argue that a concept is such a concept as we might be expected to have, the world being as it is. I have of course suggested that if action in general is analysable in terms of attributability to identifiable things, the concept would be serviceable to a spectator of phenomena. We might add, especially serviceable to any spectator who had a predilection for things which are or have bodies, and who accordingly preferred to conceive of an event as such a thing behaving in a certain way, and preferred to explain its behaviour by reference to other such things. But the vagueness of these remarks is appropriate to the grade of intellectual comfort that can be provided, and I do not pretend to improve on this as a positive account.

But something might be learned by turning the matter the other way around. It happens that if the concept of action is analysable as I propose, then our actual application of the concept is on the face of it odd. For it seems that *either* we must resort to a remarkable logical opportunism in our use of it, *or* our use of it must be protected by some extraordinary empirical facts. If it turns out that the required facts are facts, and neglected ones, our encounter with them will have lent plausibility to the analysis. The oddness arises as follows.

According to the analysis, the reports that a person raised his hand, or opened the window, like the reports that a sling raised his hand or a motor opened the window, have substantial implications for the explanation of the motion of the physical objects concerned, namely the hand and the window. They imply that it is appropriate to give the person's intentions, reasons, and the like in explanation of why the hand or the window moved.

Now it is a feature of the concept of explanation that it makes sense to speak of *the* explanation of why something is so. For anything which is relevant to the understanding of why it is so counts as part of the ideal account which we might give. We could say that the idea of *the* explanation is a regulative idea. At the same time, anything can be called the explanation which provides all we need for the purpose in hand. The regulative idea only regulates in excluding the possibility of alternative and unrelated explanations both of which explain why the same thing is so. So two accounts may each be correctly presented on their several occasions as the explanation of something, but then their tenability is subject to the possibility of fitting them together into a single account. Trivially they must be consistent with each other. But it is not enough to show them to be consistent; at least one must turn out to require the other. To illustrate this stronger requirement from the present examples, the opening of the window can be explained by the operation of the motor; if it is also the case that someone opened it to freshen the stuffy car, its opening can be explained through this purpose of his. Each account could, on the appropriate occasion, be the explanation; each can be fitted into the explanation since, on the actual occasion, causal attributability of the motion to the motor, and of the motor's operation to the switch, and of the switch's closing to a hand, was a necessary condition of attributability of the motion to the person, and hence of the appropriateness of the explanation by a purpose.

To illustrates the requirement schematically, suppose that the explanation of the fact that q is that q because p; and that the explanation is also that q because r. Both can be correct provided either that if p then r or that if r then p. Quite typically, as in the case of causal chains in which 'p', 'q', and 'r' or 'p', 'r', and 'q' report the links, it will be the case that r because p or that p because r; both these last explanations imply that in the actual circumstances p if and only if r.

The oddity which we are engaged in explaining is generated by the requirement of mutual relevance of the several explanations. But first let us for the sake of clarity set aside difficulties which arise from the weaker requirement of mutual consistency. There is a problem which needs no introduction and which is said to arise from the presence of causal explanations and from an incompatibility in principle between causal explanation and explanation in terms of intentions, purposes, reasons, and the like. Just to make clear where I stand on the problem of free will, let me remark that I have yet to be convinced by any argument to show that there is such an incompatibility *in principle*, i.e., on conceptual grounds. Still less do I see any incompatibility of this kind between explaining an action by reasons and exhaustively analysing the involvement of the body in that action into elements each of which has a causal explanation and the relations between which have causal explanations, provided that no restriction is placed on the complexity or practicability of the causal explanations. This I find fortunate, since it seems to me that this latter situation is one which we have good empirical grounds for thinking must in fact obtain. Metaphysical determinism seems to me an academic issue in the face of empirically probable physiological determinism. But neither need be regarded as threatening freedom or the presuppositions of morality until we have a better demonstration of one of these conceptual incompatibilities.

The potential difficulty which we are to explore here arises not from incompatibility in principle of two explanations, but from lack of mutual relevance. Perhaps we do not thereby leave the traditional problem of free will. To the extent that that problem has concerned, not the possibility of a causal explanation as such, but the possibility of a causal explanation totally unrelated to the explanation by reasons, it also has turned upon a difficulty of this form. Anyway, it does seem that if the physical motion of hand or window were to be explained both by the person's reasons and by causes, and if the two explanations were in principle consistent but completely unrelated, we would be forced to ask 'But which is the real explanation?' A similar crisis is provoked by the mere declaration of the appropriateness of an explanation by the person's reasons, in the presence of causal explanations, unless there is some restriction which will guarantee the mutual relation of the explanations. In other words, the very report that a person raised his hand or opened a window is potentially a rival of causal explanations of the motion of hand and window.

Many of the applications of this dictum are commonplace. We have seen how causal explanation by reference to a motor can be part of the basis for saying that a man opened a window. If the motor had been started by a short-circuit, and the short had been caused by something hitting the wires, and so on through a causal story which had nothing to do at any point with the man's body, this would be adequate ground for saying that it could not be the case that the man opened the window. When we know that a man's hand is caused to rise by the contraction of several sets of muscles, and these are caused to contract by stimulation in certain nerves, the causal account may be satisfactorily subordinate to the report of action; we have seen that we can say the muscles contracted *because* he was raising his hand (to vote on a proposal). But the moment the cause of the muscle contraction is known to be stimulation from electrodes inserted in the spine, and the causal story from there on does not return to the man's body, we are forced to say either that the man did not raise his arm or that he did so involuntarily, and in any case that he did not raise it for a reason.

In the setting of these commonplace inferences, we can begin to see the apparent logical opportunism to which I referred. This is the opportunism of the spectator who is applying the concept of action in the understanding of the effects he observes. It seems that causal relations are his constant guide. With regard to inanimate action, they are his sole concern. With regard to human action, he constantly relies upon causal chains for attributing effects in the environment to people, and constantly defers to causal chains which, by missing the body or by re-emerging from the body, show an independence which precludes attribution to a given person. But the moment a causal chain plunges deep enough into obscurity, or as a whole lies hidden under the skin, he disregards it completely. He constantly reports human actions with confidence, in ignorance of the causal explanation of the observable phenomena, even though such explanations could force him to withdraw or qualify the report. Worse, the dividing line between his deference to causal explanation and his disregard happens to be the line dividing common-sense information from common-sense ignorance; give or take a few muscles, it follows the surface of the human body.

It is a classic view that the belief in free will is an illusion due to ignorance of the causes of our choices. Here it seems that the confidence with which the ordinary concept of action is applied is due to ignorance of the causes even of our bodily movements. A corollary might be that some of the obscurantism of common sense is needed for the very use of the concept, and that the appplication of the concept ought to be undermined by awareness of successful causal explanation in both psychology and physiology.

But let us consider instead the possibility that this confidence in the absence of rival causal explanations is empirically sensible. First let us take a rough measure of common ignorance and the comparative success of scientific explanation. The relevant events are, first, human actions of the non-defective kind, which are, or are the outcome of, the settling of the question of whether to do that thing, and for which it is appropriate to seek explanations in terms of the agent's reasons; and second, bodily movements which are logically or causally required for particular actions of that kind. The relevant kind of explanation is causal, which implies that it rests upon inductively grounded principles of regularity; and we must remember that explanations of action based on what reasonable people do in certain circumstances are for that reason not causal explanations. In the case of the bodily movements, we must also specify that the causal explanation be more than the initial fragment, and be full enough to allow assessment of its dependence or independence from the agent's deliberation. Given these specifications, there is a simple summary of the empirical situation, including the results of scientific work. No such causal explanation of such an event has been successfully given in any single case.

This fact merely puts the issue in perspective. It does not justify one attitude or another to the outcome of successful causal explanation in an imaginable future. Let us ask next what empirical conjectures would have to be reasonable ones, in order for the spectator of human action to have reasonable confidence that the explanations, when available, will prove to be actually required by the agent's reasons, intentions, and the like? A general answer would be long, but there are some empirical views which have good support already and are to the point. There seems to be a very sharp discontinuity in the degree of complexity of causal explanation required for the movements of two kinds of gross physical objects, namely stones or bits of wood and the parts of the bodies of the higher animals. Further, intentions, motives, reasoning, and such things are observed to occur only in organisms which have the complexity of brain structure implied in causal explanations of the higher order of complexity. The latter view would guarantee what the former view would require, if it were to turn out that the causal explanation of a hand's rising lay in just those events in the brain which were required for a man's deciding how to vote.

The empirical discontinuity I have referred to would further make reasonable the opportunistic abandonment of causal interests at the surface of the body. A man's hand and an axe handle have so much in common, for purposes of causal inquiries, that I find I can neglect, and can rediscover with surprise, the great difference between them. What scientific advance does for us is to confirm our sense of the difference by a quantitative interpretation of it. We learn that under the skin there is an extraordinary mechanism, and that its complexity accounts for our inability in practice to give causal explanations of some of the movement's of people's bodies. Looking back, what are we to say of the naïve rules of thumb which have always prevailed in the field of application of the concept of action? These include the rules that the motion of an inanimate body generally has a physical cause of comparable grossness; that this is often so for human bodies; that sometimes, however, this is simply not so for the latter; that animals so to speak have a source of motion in themselves; that when one can find an external cause, one can never find a reason; that when one cannot find a cause, one can often find a reason; that when one cannot find a reason, one can often find a cause, I would say that as empirical rules of thumb go, these are magnificently well supported.

Suppose now that what the analysis has brought to our attention is indeed the empirical situation. Then I think we get an oblique light on the problem of free will. One needs no fondness for determinism in its most general form to feel that certain libertarian denials of it are perverse, namely those which simply declare an exception in favour of certain human actions. Why should just those events, including just those subsidiary physical events, be in principle exempt? On what principle? And yet such a libertarian doctrine constantly recurs and has a curious inherent attraction. If the present analysis of action does not gain plausibility, it at least has an extra interest, in bringing to light an empirical situation which helps to explain the appeal of such libertarian indeterminism. For the empirical situation contains an empirical analogue of indeterminism. If we are speaking of the practicability of causal explanation, and considering the world of ordinary physical objects, it is in fact a good rule that every event has a cause, except when we come to human action.

Index

Lightning Source UK Ltd.
Milton Keynes UK
UKHW030612210722
406167UK00006B/693